COURSEBOOK

Contact US!

Call center
English skills

Jane Lockwood
Hayley McCarthy

CAMBRIDGE
UNIVERSITY PRESS

CAMBRIDGE
UNIVERSITY PRESS

University Printing House, Cambridge CB2 8BS, United Kingdom

One Liberty Plaza, 20th Floor, New York, NY 10006, USA

477 Williamstown Road, Port Melbourne, VIC 3207, Australia

314–321, 3rd Floor, Plot 3, Splendor Forum, Jasola District Centre, New Delhi – 110025, India

79 Anson Road, #06–04/06, Singapore 079906

Cambridge University Press is part of the University of Cambridge.

It furthers the University's mission by disseminating knowledge in the pursuit of education, learning and research at the highest international levels of excellence.

www.cambridge.org
Information on this title: www.cambridge.org/9780521124737

First published 2010

20 19 18 17 16 15 14 13 12 11 10 9 8 7 6 5 4 3 2

Printed in the United Kingdom by Latimer Trend

ISBN 978-0-521-12473-7 paperback Coursebook color edition with Audio CD
ISBN 978-0-521-17858-7 paperback Trainer's Manual

Information regarding prices, travel timetables and other factual information given in this work are correct at the time of first printing but Cambridge University Press does not guarantee the accuracy of such information thereafter.

Authors' notes

Authoring credits

Steven Finch

Philippe Malin

Many thanks to both for their substantial contributions in writing sections of the coursebook, as well as their inspiration and support throughout the project.

Acknowledgments

Contact US! would not have been possible without the work and support of a number of colleagues and family members. First, we would like to acknowledge the company who worked on this project collaboratively: FuturePerfect. We would also like to thank the People2Outsource team, most particularly Vincent Bautista and Juan Miguel Brion, whose work piloting the course gave us invaluable insights into the call center trainer's experience of teaching these materials.

We would like to thank Neil Elias who provided early data for research into the nature of call center interaction. This coursebook would never have been possible without his support and advice on what the call center industry is really looking for in good customer communication. To Dan Elias, who inspired "Dan and Dora" and who tirelessly and patiently proofread, listened, and contributed.

Lastly, to all our friends and colleagues at Cambridge University Press. Thanks go out to the Hong Kong Cambridge University Press office for gallantly hosting so many working meetings and for their work on the *Contact US!* website. To Chris Boughton for his commitment to getting the coursebook started … and for the title! To Josep Mas as Publishing Manager, whose patience and attention to detail kept us all on track; and to Project Manager Chris Caridia, whose thoroughness and care have been essential to the success of this project.

Plan of the book

	A The call	B Focus on language	C Soft skills
Unit 1 Being clear and polite *Pages 2–12*	• Franchise inquiry	• Forming questions in spoken English • Open and closed questions • American idioms (1)	• Explaining information clearly • Putting the customer on hold
Unit 2 Predicting customer need *Pages 13–24*	• Bulk buy inquiry	• Present continuous (1) • Using *just* • Phrasal verbs (1)	• Predicting caller need • Backchanneling
Unit 3 Explaining and giving instructions *Pages 25–34*	• Caller changing phone number	• Zero conditional • Giving instructions using imperatives and softeners • Using idioms	• Giving clear instructions and explanations
Unit 4 Defusing anger *Pages 35–45*	• Extra charges on bill	• Modal verbs • Phrasal verbs (2)	• Defusing anger • Sounding sincere
Unit 5 Probing for information and admitting mistakes *Pages 46–57*	• Camera repair	• The interrupted past • The second conditional • American idioms (2)	• Probing questions • Admitting mistakes
Unit 6 Dealing with complaints and checking information *Pages 58–68*	• Unexplained text messages on monthly invoice	• Modals used to express obligation • Passives • Phrasal verbs (3)	• Active listening • Checking information
Unit 7 Showing empathy *Pages 69–80*	• Complaint about termination of policy	• Present continuous (2) • Extended use of *just, actually,* and *still* • Modals used in polite requests • Phrasal verbs (4)	• Evaluating the agent • Building relationships • Showing empathy
Unit 8 Thinking aloud and building solidarity *Pages 81–89*	• Connecting to the Internet	• Modals of ability • Using the first conditional for instructions	• Thinking aloud professionally • Building solidarity through the pronouns *we* and *us*
Unit 9 Keeping control of an aggressive call *Pages 90–100*	• Insurance policy complaint	• Expressing regret • Making comparisons • Idioms and phrasal verbs	• Keeping control of an aggressive call • Sounding "robotic"
Unit 10 Dealing with sarcasm *Pages 101–110*	• Invoice in the wrong name	• Conditional sentence rules – and how to break them • Modals with several functional meanings • Active and passive forms • American idioms (3)	• Dealing with conflict • Responding to sarcasm

D Pronunciation	E Read and explain	F Intercultural matters	G Role-play
• Rising intonation • Falling intonation • Syllabus stress • Consonant clusters	• Franchise information	• Geography of the United States • Retirement in the United States	• Explaining to a prospective franchisee
• Contractions • /s/ or /z/	• Animal colic	• American farming and ranch culture • Customer expectations: "thinking outside the box"	• Deciding whether to give a refund
• Connected speech	• How to use a hands-free headset	• Cultural differences • Stereotypes • Public and private information • Gathering private information	• Helping a caller set up an Internet connection
• Understanding and using intonation to express emotions	• Canceling the Axe Credit Card	• Money matters in American culture • Taking responsibility and understanding blame and accountability	• Deciding whether to escalate
• Silent consonants • Silent syllables	• Guide to choosing a first camera	• Higher education • Family ties	• Deciding whether to replace a customer's defective equipment
• Word stress and meaning (1)	• Summarizing a letter of complaint	• Humor • Friendly or furious? (understanding sarcasm) • Responding to humor	• Dealing with an angry caller
• Differentiating vowel sounds (1)	• Getting a visa	• Litigation and compensation culture • Dealing with customer dissatisfaction	• Sorting out the problems of a dissatisfied customer
• Intonation when giving instructions • Intonation and context	• Giving information about an IT company	• Diagnosing self-reliant customers • Self-empowerment culture	• Giving a caller technical instructions
• Word stress and meaning (2)	• Giving information about making a car insurance claim	• Direct answers to direct questions • Saying *no*	• Regaining the trust of an angry caller
• Differentiating vowel sounds (2)	• Retelling a story	• Women's independence • Multiculturalism and the American Dream	• Apologizing and regaining a caller's trust

SELF EVALUATION

1 Being clear and polite

What you will learn!

At the end of this unit, you will have covered:

A The call: listening to understand the purpose and details of the call, as well as the feelings of the caller

B Focus on language: asking questions ◆ common idioms in American English

C Soft skills: putting customers on hold and responding to emotional cues

D Pronunciation: intonation patterns when questioning ◆ stresses and vowel sounds.

E Read and explain: reading, analyzing and synthesizing information in order to give clear explanations

F Intercultural matters: USA geography ◆ cultural issues related to retirement

G Role-play: simulating a call center transaction

DAN and DORA: WELCOME TO THE CALL CENTER!

WELCOME TO THE TEAM. I'LL BE YOUR MENTOR AS YOU'RE SETTLING IN.

JUST BE CLEAR AND POLITE. I'LL BE RIGHT HERE ALL THE TIME.

THANKS. I THINK I'LL NEED LOTS OF HELP.

A The call

1 Pre-listening activity

The caller says "I've always wanted to open an Atlantic coffee shop."
What do you think the call will be about?

2 Global listening activity

Now listen to the call. As you listen to it for the first time, note down information about:

1. Who is talking to whom?

2. What is the main purpose of the call?

Discuss your answers in groups.

3 Detailed listening activity

Listen to the call again. Then look at the statements below and decide whether they are true (T) or false (F).

1. The caller is feeling very anxious about opening a coffee shop. ....

2. The caller already owns a coffee shop and has been operating it for two years. ....

3. The agent says he needs to contact a rep to get an application form. ....

4. The agent is helpful and polite. ....

5. The agent is efficient. ....

6. There is no website available for the caller to find out about Atlantic Aroma coffee shop franchises. ....

7. The agent says the caller will make a success of opening a coffee shop. ....

8. The rep will explain the details of the Atlantic Aroma coffee shop franchise when he/she calls. ....

○ *Compare your answers with your partner/group. Your trainer will provide the correct answers. Listen again for those answers that were not correct.*

B Focus on language

1 Forming questions in spoken English

■ In spoken English, we take a lot of "short cuts." For example, when we ask questions, we often rely on rising intonation (when your voice pitch gets higher) to show that we are asking questions, rather than using the full grammatically correct question form. These short cuts make speaking efficient and help communication.

1 *Write in the full grammatically correct version of each question. Compare your answer with your partner.*

Short-cut question form	Full grammatical question form
Or you already have one?	*Do you already have one?*
And you just want to brand it Atlantic?	
OK, you wanna do that?	
Your first name?	
Your phone number?	
You get it?	

2 Open and closed questions

It is important in call center transactions to be able to ask the right questions in the correct way, particularly when the caller has a complicated problem that needs resolving. There are three main types of questions:

- **Open questions:** These require a response that contains information or details. Open questions are sometimes called *wh* questions because they start with *what, where, when, who, as well as how*. These questions are useful on the phone when you are probing for information. *wh* questions are formed with WH(AT) + auxiliary + subject pronoun + main verb: *What + did + you + say?*

- **Closed questions:** These questions require a "yes" or "no" answer. They are useful on the phone for checking information. They are formed with AUXILIARY (*do / did / can*, etc.) + subject pronoun + main verb: *Did + you + say + that … ?*

- **Question tags:** Another form of a closed question is the question tag: *You said that … didn't you?* These questions are useful also for checking and confirming information with the caller. They are formed with the subject pronoun and auxiliary (*isn't, haven't, can't*, etc.) or *don't / didn't*.

1 *Complete the dialog below by using open or closed question forms.*

Martha is feeling a little anxious!

Agent: Good evening. This is Ken, ...

Caller: Yes, I've lost my credit card and maybe someone has stolen it. I was out shopping and I used it yesterday, but …

Agent: *OK, let me take a few details and I'll do my best to help you. Can I take your name and Social Security number?*

Caller: Yes, my name is Martha Lewis and my Social Security is 378 59 2300.

Agent: .... ?

Caller: Well, it might have been stolen and that's what I'm afraid of …

Agent: .... ?

Caller: Yes, I've just been looking in the normal places. You know – bedroom, under the bed. That's where I always keep my money, you know.

Agent: .... ?

Caller: Just a couple of days ago when I went to the supermarket. I spent about $125 on groceries.

Agent: .... ?

Caller: Oh, I hadn't thought about that. Perhaps I should go back and check there.

Agent: .... ?

Caller: Oh, you never know, and last night I went out with a couple of friends and my bag zipper was open when I left the bar. It was a bit strange, but I didn't think anything was stolen. But now I'm worried, I think I should report it stolen, just in case. You know, be on the safe side.

Agent: .... ?

Caller: No, I'll go back to the supermarket and if it's not there I'll give you another call.

Agent: .... ?

Caller: OK, that sounds like a good idea. A temporary stop would be good. Just so no one can run up my credit!

Agent: .... ?

Caller: 84692672057

Agent: .... ?

Caller: Social Security is 378 59 2300.

Agent: .... ?

Caller: April 10th, 1969.

Agent: OK, that's all done, it's on temporary hold. And give me a call tomorrow. I really hope you find it, Martha. Thank you for calling.

Caller: Thanks, bye.

2 *Look at your answers to Activity 1. Discuss which ones you think can be shortened.*
Write five full questions and five shortened questions.

Short-cut question form	Full grammatical question form

3 American idioms (1)

1 *Look at the idioms below and match them to the best meaning. Some of them are taken from the call you have just listened to.*

Idiom	Meaning
1. just bear with me for a sec	a) good at business
2. to go under	b) to assist or help
3. and stuff like that	c) getting involved
4. to get a feel for	d) to understand
5. to bite off more than you can chew	e) to take on too much
6. getting yourself into	f) and other things
7. to give a hand	g) to be unsuccessful in business
8. an old hand at this	h) to be experienced
9. to have a business head	i) to wait for a moment

2 *Now list any idioms you know that include the word "head". What do they mean?*

Idiomatic expression	Meaning
heads up	warning
head over heels in love	very much in love

C Soft skills

1 Explaining information clearly

- Many call center interactions are focused on explaining policies or procedures and providing information about services and products. If a customer calls with a problem or is confused about a product or service, giving him/her clear explanations is a vital part of providing good service.

- Agents often have difficulty in providing clear explanations because they need to give the customer information in a way that is often different to the agents' first language. English speakers from the Western world tend to speak in a *linear* and *logical* manner. They also expect questions to be answered directly and instantly. They dislike answers which are seen as avoiding the question or "beating about the bush."

- If a customer calls up and is upset that his/her book order has not arrived yet and wants to know the reason, he/she will expect the agent to tell him/her immediately what has happened, and then follow it up with reasons or explanations.

- Practicing direct logical explanations is a very useful skill to help you to attain customer satisfaction!

1 *Read this agent's clear explanation of how to apply for a franchise and the notes below:*

OK, well the way that it works is that we take down your information, we email you a template, you have to fill it out and then fax it to the number at the top, and then the rep contacts you within seven days.

Notes:

1. Words which show the order things are done, such as *then*.
2. Use of parallel structures: *we do this*, *you do that*.
3. Use of present simple tense to show the information is an established fact or procedure: *we take down your information*.
4. Stress of important content words, such as *template*.

2 *Work with a partner and choose one of the topics below. Spend two minutes planning on your scratchpad and then sit back-to-back and make your explanations to each other as clearly as possible.*

- Why education is important for society.
- Why pet animals should be vaccinated against rabies.
- What are the most important qualities for a good leader to have?

2 Putting the customer on hold

How do customers feel when they are put on hold? The more time that passes where they are left completely unattended, the less confidence they have that their problem will be dealt with. Here are some simple guidelines:

- Tell the customer that you will put him/her on hold. Say why and for how long:
  Mr. Thomas, I'm going to put you on hold for a short time to find out the answer to your question.
  OR
  Mr. Thomas, would it be OK if I put you on hold for a minute so I can go and find out the answer to your question?

- If it is taking longer than you anticipated, go back to the customer and let him/her know you are still there and working on the problem:
  Hello, Mr. Thomas, are you still there? I just need another minute.

- When you return, thank the customer for holding on and deliver your message:
  Thank you very much for holding, Mr. Thomas. I'm pleased to be able to say …

In pairs, practice the following two scenarios. Take turns being the agent and the customer.

Scenario 1
Your customer has asked you a very complicated question about a product. There is nothing on your system that explains it, so you need to talk to your supervisor. This customer is feeling frustrated at the beginning of the call because his problem has meant he cannot use the product.

Scenario 2
Your customer is angry and wants his/her call escalated to the supervisor. You try to placate the caller, but without much success. You decide to put the caller on hold in order to locate a supervisor, although your real agenda is to give the customer time to "cool down", as the problem does not warrant escalation.

D Pronunciation

■ **Rising and falling intonation: what they tell you**
Often in English when we ask a question, we raise our intonation (our voice pitch gets higher) at the end of the question. This invites the listener to respond. Generally speaking, rising intonation will invite a response and will keep the interaction going. Falling intonation, on the other hand, will close the conversation.

1 Rising intonation: asking questions and opening up interaction

1 *Look at the questions below and practice rising intonation with your partner.*

   1. **A:** It's not working. I've wasted about three hours trying this.
        B: Really? How many times have you tried to log on this morning?
        A: About 10 times. It's frustrating.

   2. **A:** Did you get that?
        B: I'm sorry, I didn't quite catch that. What is your name and address?
        A: It's Bill Hudson, 55 Oakwood Drive, Phoenix, Arizona.

   3. **A:** When are you going to Houston?
        B: The day after next. Why do you ask?
        A: Oh, OK. Then you'll be able to come to the conference tomorrow.

   4. **A:** It's been sent already. You should have it now.
        B: Really? No, I don't have it yet. When did you send it?

   5. **A:** You need to get here right away.
        B: Oh, no! What time is the meeting?
        A: In about 30 minutes.

 2 *Now listen to the call again. Write down five questions you hear that use rising intonation.*

2 Falling intonation: closing down an interaction

1 *Look at the sentences below and practice using falling intonation with your partner.*

   1. So that's settled then.
   2. Please accept my apologies about this.
   3. I hope this doesn't happen again.
   4. We look forward to it.
   5. I'm sure you understand.

 2 *Now go back to the transcript and listen to the questions. Write down five more statements that use falling intonation.*

3 Syllable stress

■ An important part of speaking clearly is using the correct syllable stress in words. To be accurate, you must first be sure that you are able to identify the number of syllables in a word before the stressed syllable can be indentified:
A|ME|ri|ca has four syllables and the second syllable is stressed.
BA|si|cly has three syllables (although it is commonly mispronounced with four syllables). The first syllable is stressed.

 1 *Listen to the state names in Additional Listening and identify the number of syllables and the stressed syllable in that word.*

STATE	Number of syllables	Stressed syllable
1. Arkansas	3	AR|kan|sas
2. California	4	Cal|i|FOR|nia
3. Connecticut		
4. Florida		
5. Georgia		
6. Illinois		
7. Louisiana		
8. Massachusetts		
9. Michigan		
10. Mississippi		
11. Missouri		
12. New Jersey		
13. New York		
14. North Dakota		
15. Ohio		
16. Pennsylvania		
17. Tennessee		
18. Texas		
19. Virginia		
20. Wisconsin		

4 Consonant clusters

■ Consonant clusters are consonant sounds that appear next to one another. Pronouncing one consonant sound and immediately following it with another can be difficult. Look at this example:
Alaska The consonant cluster here is /sk/. The two sounds blend together, and there is no pause or break: Ala-ska. The /s/ sound here blends into the /k/ like in the word *sky* or *ski*.

1 *Now go back and look at the American states again and underline all the consonant clusters. Read them aloud.*

 2 *Now choose part of the call and listen to it for consonant clusters. Write down ten examples.*

E Read and explain

○ *Spend one minute skimming the text below, then complete the paired activities.*

FRANCHISE INFORMATION
Day Spa Dreams

10 STEPS TO YOUR DAY SPA DREAMS

1. Complete the Franchise Application Form (FAF) and send it to Spa Horizon, P. O. Box 7445, Arizona, 75031, USA.

2. Once your application has been approved, you will be invited to a full-day seminar to discuss the benefits of owning a Spa Horizon franchise. At that seminar, we'll assign you a "franchise mentor," who will assist you with every step of the franchise development.

3. On completion of the seminar and the assignment of your own mentor, we will send a *Franchise Offer Circular (FOC)*, which outlines all the rights and obligations of the franchisee.

4. You then sign the *Acknowledgment of Receipt (AR)* and send it back in the envelope provided.

5. You visit a Spa Horizon of your choice and spend a full day experiencing the products and services. You will also meet key management personnel for a 60-minute question-and-answer forum.

6. You will then be asked to send a short video presentation into our headquarters in New York outlining your vision statement and presenting your business plan.

7. The Board of Spa Horizons will then let you know within 2 weeks if you will be awarded the franchise opportunity.

8. If you are awarded the franchise, you will sign the *Spa Horizon Franchise Agreement (SHFA)* and pay the initial Franchise Fee. We recommend that you get your lawyer to go through the document.

9. You then start looking for a location for your Spa Horizon, and you work with your mentor to begin the start-up process.

10. All publicity materials need to be cleared with Spa Horizon head office, and then you are free to open your doors!

Regular annual forums are held in all states to ensure all franchisees can get together and share the experience of being part of the Spa Horizon family!

1   *Student A is the agent. Explain to the caller clearly and concisely in your own words how to apply for a franchise without reading directly from the text.*

2   *Swap roles. The agent answers the following inquiry.*
    Caller: Is franchizing a long and complicated process? How much support do I get, and do I get a chance to use my own ideas?

F Intercultural matters

1 Geography of the United States

1 *Have any of you ever traveled to the United States? What were your impressions? If you haven't, where would you like to go?*

2 *In pairs, decide on a listener and a speaker, then sit back-to-back. The listener closes his/her book and looks at a blank map your trainer will give him/her. The speaker looks at the map in the book and describes to the listener the position of each of the U.S. states in alphabetical order. After five minutes, check how many are correctly labeled.*

3 *Was the size or geographic position of any of the states surprising to you?*

2 Retirement in the United States

1 *Think about retirement in your country. How do retired people expect to be treated? What do they expect to do with their lives?*

2 *In pairs, look at the table below. Read the information on retirement in the United States and compare it with your own country.*

Aspects of retirement	United States	Your country
Age	Typically 65. The average range is 55–70.	
Pensions	When U.S. citizens retire, they receive a monthly income (pension) from Social Security deposits. This income is created because every year of employment a contribution is made to Social Security. It is returned to them upon retirement, plus interest. The larger their contribution is, the larger their retirement package will be.	
Where is home?	Generally, when people retire, they remain financially independent because they have a retirement income. This means that they continue to live alone or with their spouse. Retirement homes are another option for those who need nursing or other kinds of day-to-day care. In less common cases, the retired person who needs care will live with family members who will provide financial support and physical care themselves.	

Aspects of retirement	United States	Your country
Being a "burden"	There is a commonly held belief and fear among retired people in the U.S. that if they need help from their families at this point in their lives, they will be a "burden". This is considered a very bad thing, and it is typical for elderly people who are in need of care and support to refuse such help for this reason.	
Realizing dreams	Some people consider retirement to be an opportunity to realize dreams or aspirations that were not possible when they were working to support their families. This is an empowering feeling and is linked to the American Dream. The American Dream is the belief that an average person can achieve extraordinary things. Many pursue their ambitions during retirement. This can mean that they do not really retire from work!	

3 Discussion:

1. What do you think are the most important differences between the U.S. and your country?
2. Are there any other aspects of retirement that you think should be added to the table?
3. What would you like to do when you retire?
4. Has your understanding of Americans changed after learning about retirement there?

 4 Listen to the call again. In pairs, brainstorm adjectives to describe the caller. Include what you think the caller's attitude toward retirement is.

G Role-play

○ **Read through the following scenario and rolecards carefully. Then act out the role play.**

Scenario

A young graduate is inquiring about the possibility of opening a health spa under a brand based in the United States called Spa Horizons. This brand is extremely well known and provides high-quality beauty treatments to mainly middle-class women, although there appears to be a growing market for men, particularly in West and East Coast cities. The checks on prospective franchisees are thorough. They are required to give full details on the amount of investment, location, qualified staff, and previous experience.

ROLECARD 1

The customer (prospective franchisee)

You are a young graduate in business management, and hospitality and tourism. You are very interested in the health tourism and in beauty treatments like spa, massage, and cosmetic treatments. You want to start up your own business and have just inherited an investment amount (US$250,000) from your grandmother. You did an internship with Spa Horizon in Los Angeles in your final year of college and enjoyed it. You are thinking of starting up a branch in Boston and have already been looking for sites to rent. You want to know what criteria you must fullfill in order to get a franchise and open up.

ROLECARD 2

The agent dealing with Spa Horizon franchises

You have received an inquiry from a prospective franchisee. You need to fill out the form on the next page and make an evaluation of whether this caller is worth following up. Comments on the suitability of this prospective franchisee are important for the head office so they know whether it is worthwhile pursuing an application.

Spa Horizon INQUIRY FORM

Name: ....

Gender: ....   Age: ....

Address: ....

Phone: ....   Email: ....

Qualification: ....

Relevant experience: ....

Investment prospect: ....

Recommendation: Yes ☐   No ☐

H Self-evaluation

Tasks	Check	Comments (areas for self-improvement)
A The call Did you understand the purpose of the call and the detailed information with particular reference to the caller's emotion?	☐	
B Focus on language Can you ask different kinds of questions and use more American idioms?	☐	
C Soft skills Do you feel more confident about making clear explanations? How do you feel about putting your caller on hold?	☐	
D Pronunciation Do you feel your intonation has improved when asking questions? How confident are you with pronouncing American state names?	☐	
E Read and explain Can you read, synthesize, and then clearly explain to someone what you have read?	☐	
F Intercultural matters Do you feel more confident about the geography of the USA? Do you feel you have learned something about how Americans view work and retirement?	☐	
G Role-play For this unit overall, what were your strengths and weaknesses?		

2 Predicting customer need

What you will learn!
At the end of this unit, you will have covered:

A The call: listening to understand the overall purpose and details of the call, as well as the feelings of the caller

B Focus on language: using the present continuous ◆ some common phrasal verbs ◆ using *just* when communicating with a customer

C Soft skills: predicting customer need ◆ giving feedback to the customer *(backchanneling)*

D Pronunciation: contracted forms

E Read and explain: reading and synthesizing information about animal medicine to explain to a customer in non-technical English

F Intercultural matters: using customer information to practice "thinking outside the box"

G Role-play: simulating a call center transaction about returning a television

DAN and DORA IN THE CALL CENTER CAFE

TODAY A CUSTOMER WANTED ME TO GO AGAINST COMPANY POLICY!

I SAID IT WASN'T POSSIBLE. HE TRIED TO ESCALATE, BUT I STOOD MY GROUND!

OK, BUT YOU CAN SOMETIMES MAKE EXCEPTIONS. THEN THE CUSTOMER FEELS LISTENED TO AND CARED FOR.

IT'S FINE, YOU'RE STILL LEARNING!

A The call

1 Pre-listening activity

The caller says "I don't want to mess around with small amounts. Waste of time."
What do you think the call will be about?

2 Global listening activity

Listen to the call and check the sentence that best describes the main purpose of the call.

1. The call is about a customer complaining that his animals are dying of colic. .... ☐
2. The call is about a customer trying to find out if he can buy a large amount of Colixin. .... ☐
3. The call is about the outlets in Denver that may sell Colixin. .... ☐

3 Detailed listening activity

Answer the questions below and write two new questions of your own for a partner to answer.
Compare answers with your partner and listen again for those answers that were not correct.

Questions	Answers
1. Where is the caller from?	
2. What is the caller's problem?	
3. Where can Colixin be bought from?	
4. Does the company do direct sales to the consumer?	
5. How is the caller feeling by the end of the call?	
6. How would you rate this call?	
7. _____ ?	
8. _____ ?	

B Focus on language

1 Present continuous (1)

■ We use the present continuous to talk about …

♦ something that is happening at the actual time of speaking:
They're leaving the airport now.

♦ future arrangements or with *going to* to talk about future plans:
We're meeting tomorrow at 10 a.m.
We're going to deduct the amount from your account at the end of the month.

♦ something that is in progress, but not actually happening at the time of speaking:
I'm reading this interesting book about call centers.

■ Some verbs are not normally used in the continuous tense. These verbs usually relate to feelings:
like, love, hate, understand.

1 *Look at the transcript and underline all the examples of the present continuous used to talk about something in progress at the time of speaking.*

2 *Complete the sentences below with the present continuous (are doing) or the present simple (do).*

1. They .... *are eating* .... (eat) dinner this evening at TGF's.
2. I .... (love) to shop at the big malls on the weekends.
3. We .... (not understand) the instructions for logging in when we are traveling.
4. Sorry, you can't speak to her. She .... (talk) on the other line.
5. We .... (know) over 500 Chinese characters already.
6. You .... (think) it's a bad idea?

2 Using *just*

■ Both the customer and the agent use the word *just* regularly. Why do they choose this word? Because it helps us …
   ◆ to emphasize and simplify:
      The cost is just $5!
      You just need to call this number.
   ◆ to express that an action has been very recently completed, or is about to be completed:
      I just called him.
      I'm just about to call him.

1 *The examples below are taken from the transcript. Put (S) where just simplifies or emphasizes the message, and (C) when it describes a completed action or one about to be completed.*

1. I'm **just** inquiring about Colixin. .... | S |
2. I'll **just** check some information. .... | |
3. I **just** came back from seeing him. .... | |
4. I'll **just** give you the list of our outlets. .... | |
5. You can **just** talk to the store manager. .... | |

2 *Now answer these requests from customers. Use just in your answers.*

1. I'm still waiting for that contract. Have you sent it yet? It's been over a month.
2. Can you explain to me again how I can access my voicemail on my new phone?
3. Where have you been? I've been waiting on the phone for over 20 minutes!
4. Can I speak to your supervisor?

3 Phrasal verbs (1)

■ A phrasal verb is formed when a common verb is followed by one (or sometimes two) prepositions: *add up, come down with.*

■ The meaning of a phrasal verb is usually different from the meaning of just the verb and the preposition separately. For example, *be run down* means "to feel unwell due to exhaustion."

I'M FEELING REALLY RUN DOWN.

MAYBE YOU'RE COMING DOWN WITH SOMETHING. WHY DON'T YOU TAKE A BREAK?

1 *Choose the best phrasal verb to complete the sentences below.*

| come up with | come into | come over | come down with | come across |

1. He (presents himself) .... as a very arrogant person.
2. They always (visit us) .... on Saturday nights.
3. The animals have (become sick) .... colic.
4. The employees (thought of) .... new ways of doing the work in less time.
5. The boys (inherited) .... a million dollars from their grandparents.

2 *Now find some more examples of phrasal verbs in the transcript.*

C Soft skills

1 Predicting caller need

- When a customer calls, he/she is usually in need of something. It may be something of high importance (a lost credit card), or it may be of lesser importance (a call to provide a change of address). Whatever the need, the call is important to the customer, and he/she wants to be properly understood.

- A good listener understands the information and the different feelings of the communicator well enough to predict his/her needs. For the agent, it means being two steps ahead; for the caller, it feels like heaven!

- Useful language for predicting caller need:

  It sounds to me like you really need to …
  I wonder if it's possible to …
  I don't know for sure, but we could try …
  It may be worth contacting …
  How about we try … ?

1 *Look at the excerpt from the call. Work with a partner and improve the agent's response.*

Caller:
We're going to use one cup a week or one cup every two weeks. Now, as I said, in my herd we've got over 50, and we're going to use it on all of them. I wonder if we can get it in bulk and how big? And how much?

Caller meant:
SMALL AMOUNTS OF COLOXIN ARE NO GOOD BECAUSE OF THE AMOUNT INVOLVED AND THE EXPENSE OF BUYING THE MEDICINE THAT WAY. COMMERCIAL OUTLETS WILL BE NO GOOD, SO I NEED TO KNOW WHERE THE SOURCE IS.

Agent:
OK. Are you able to hold for a moment? I'll just check some information about this … Thank you very much for waiting. OK, with regard to this … you can only buy the Colixin product from our main outlets on the stock list, OK?

2 *Look at the comments below. You are the agent. Write what the caller meant (the "hidden message"), and then give a response that takes into account the hidden message and your understanding of caller need.*

1. I'm calling because I'm stuck in the worst traffic jam in Tokyo, and my flight leaves in 30 minutes and I have a really important meeting in New York City tomorrow morning.

   Caller means: ....

   Your response: ....

2. I bought a new cell phone last week and I accidentally put it through the washing machine!

   Caller means: ....

   Your response: ....

3. Oh, dear, I've just finished all the accounts on an Excel file, and the computer screen has gone blue!

   Caller means: ....

   Your response: ....

4. I've just discovered that my credit card is missing. This is the second time this month. I don't use it and it's more bother than it's worth!

   Caller means: ....

   Your response: ....

5. My grandmother lives in Alaska. She loves gardening but has to stay indoors right now because it's snowing. It's her birthday in two days, and I want to get her something special.

   Caller means: ....

   Your response: ....

2 Backchanneling

- *Backchanneling* means letting someone know that you are paying attention to him/her. In practice it means giving verbal feedback throughout the listening period of a conversation with short responses such as *uh* and *um*, or slightly longer responses that simply acknowledge what has been said.

- Backchanneling can be in response to a specific statement:
  Caller: All I did was put the batteries in and the whole device exploded in my face!
  Agent: Oh no! The whole device exploded?

- Or it can simply be to show that you are continuing to listen and understand:
  Caller: So I went to the doctor …
  Agent: Uh-huh.
  Caller: … and he said …

- Callers from the U.S. are typically in need of verbal or semi-verbal responses. When an American over the phone says *Oh no, I've spilled my drink!* or *Now where did I put that form?*, he/she expects some kind of response from you. Often a simple *oh!* or *ah* will suffice.

- Sometimes backchanneling means repeating what the caller has said back to him/her:
  Caller: Can you buy it in bulk?
  Agent: Can you buy it in bulk? Well, …
  The agent then goes on to probe further. You don't always have to repeat word for word what the customer says, but try to use language which will let the caller know that you heard him/her.

- The opposite of backchanneling is silence or "dead air." If you are silent, your American customers might feel you are not listening or not competent enough to handle their situation.

1 *Work in pairs. Student A tells a story (2–3 minutes) about a time when he/she was embarrassed. Student B listens the first time in silence. Student A tells the story again. This time Student B should give backchanneling responses. Change roles and do it again. How did you both feel? Discuss how silence and backchanneling might make a customer feel.*

2 *Listen to the calls from Units 1 and 2 again and note down examples of backchanneling.*

3 *Work in pairs. Compare your notes on the two calls:*

- ◆ Were there any differences in terms of backchanneling?
- ◆ Were there differences in the way the calls ended?
- ◆ Which caller is happier?
- ◆ Which call is better for business?

4 *Work with a partner to provide backchanneling responses to these callers.*

1. I'm sick and tired of calling! Can you please fix the spelling of my name on the correspondence?
2. Good morning. I'm inquiring about the application process for an auto loan.
3. Hi there. I'm a little confused about this application form. Can you walk me through it?
4. Yeah, I'm calling about my latest invoice. How did you come up with it? I'm not paying this!
5. Connect me to your supervisor right away!

D Pronunciation

1 Contractions

- ◼ A contraction is two words combined to make a shorter sound: *I have > I've …*

- ◼ A common mistake with contractions is to leave out the shortened sound in the second word - for example: *I* instead of *I've*. If you don't pronounce contractions correctly, you can confuse your listener! Look at the difference in meaning in these sentences:

I like peace and quiet. (a general liking for peace and quiet)

I'd like peace and quiet. (a wish for peace and quiet now)

Contracted form	Full form	Examples
'll	will	*She'll be late. I'll send it.*
's	is/has	*It's good. He's eaten.*
're	are	*They're away. You're tall.*
'd	would/had	*We'd like to. You'd better.*
've	have	*I've been there. We've left.*
n't	not	*He didn't go. I wasn't sure.*

 1 *Listen to the call again and note down all the contractions. Compare your notes with a partner. Check your answers against the transcript.*

 2 *Listen to these contracted forms in Additional Listening. Then, in pairs, practice saying them aloud in a sentence.*

it's	there's	they're	we've	we'll	I'll	you'll	aren't	that's

3 *Look at the sentences below and explain the different meanings of the two versions.*

1. a) It's closed.
    b) It closed.

2. a) We're married.
    b) We married.

3. a) He's always played musical instruments.
    b) He always played musical instruments.

4. a) I'd like to have tea with you.
    b) I like to have tea with you.

2 /s/ or /z/

■ The contracted form of both *is* and *has* is *'s*. However, the letter *s* can sound like /s/ or /z/ depending on the sound before:
It's … /s/ after *p, t, k, f,* and *th*
He's … /z/ after all vowels and all other consonants

1 *Write example sentences to demonstrate the rules above.*

p	*Our ship's gone.*
m	
l	
th	
e	
f	
r	
a	

2 *Circle all the contracted forms of* is *and* has *in the transcript and decide if the pronunciation is /s/ or /z/.*
Work in pairs and read them aloud.

E Read and explain

○ *Work in pairs. Student A (the agent) spends one minute reading the text. Student B (the farmer) reads the farmer profile. Student A extracts key information from the text to assist B. Then change roles. This time Student B is the agent and Student A is a pet owner.*

ANIMAL HOSPITAL

Many animal lovers and farmers worry when their pets and livestock are clearly in pain because of colic. Our vet at Colixin has provided some answers to frequently asked questions about animal colic.

What is colic?
Many vets, farmers, and horse owners complain that colic is very prevalent in cows and horses in particular, and it strikes all ages and all breeds. Colic is a general term which describes the disruption of the animal's normal intestinal processes, and can range from quite mild to very severe. In some cases colic can be life-threatening to the animal, although this is rare. Sometimes farmers may confuse colic for other conditions such as foaling and kidney or bladder problems.

There are many different types of colic, but the most common type is called spasmodic colic. Spasmodic colic occurs when the intestines become overactive.

What are the symptoms of colic?
Animals are like babies: they can't tell you where it hurts. Usually the animals lose their appetite and keep trying to "scratch" their stomachs with their hind legs. They appear distracted and in pain, and very sensitive to touch.

What causes colic?
There can be a number of causes of colic, although it is not contagious. It can be caused by inadequate de-worming procedures, teeth problems, or even changes in exercise patterns. The animal usually appears to be in sudden and dramatic pain. However, this type of colic usually responds effectively and quickly to medication.

Another cause is dietary and eating patterns. Sudden changes in diet, irregular eating, overeating, and speed of eating will all have a negative impact on the animal's digestive tract.

How can colic be best treated?
Most cases can be treated by administering medication, and about 5% of cases require surgery. Those animals that can be treated with medication have a much better prognosis than those which require surgical intervention.

What is Colixin?
Colixin has been developed by a team of vets and pharmacists who have wide experience in treating animals with this condition. It is safe and there appear to be no side effects to administering Colixin.

Farmer profile
Two years ago you lost a lot of your cattle (and a lot of money) to foot and mouth disease. You feel very anxious about the fact that two of your cows have developed colic. You have just called the Colixin hotline with the following questions:

- Is colic contagious?

- What's the best treatment for it? Does the medication always work?

- Do you think the fact that we changed the horses' food from maize to straw last month may have caused it?

Pet owner profile
You have a Shetland pony called Goldilocks. She has lost her appetite and seems to be in pain. She keeps trying to scratch the side of her abdomen with her hoof. You want to ask the following questions:

- Do you think this could be colic? What else could it be?

- If I give her Colixin, how long will it take to help her? Is it safe?

- Is she going to die?

F Intercultural matters

1 American farming and ranch culture

■ There are many "micro" cultures in the United States. In this section, you will learn about American farming and ranch culture and how to use this information to provide better customer service.

1 *Read the information about agricultural workers below. But remember that not every farmer will fit this profile, so you must keep an open mind when taking a call.*

Who are agricultural workers in the USA?

Workforce
- Agriculture directly employs 2% of America's workforce, compared to 57% in India, 64% in China, 31% in the Philippines, and 18% in Costa Rica.
- Agriculture is a male-dominated industry (approx. 80%).
- Workers in the agricultural industry typically have low education levels. Nearly 25% don't finish high school.

Facts and figures
- Earnings are generally below average income.
- Dominant farming states include: Iowa, Nebraska, Idaho, North Dakota, Wyoming, Arkansas, and Montana.
- Politics: electoral results over the last 20 years show that most farming states consistently vote Republican.
- 98% of farms and ranches are family owned.
- Religion: the dominant religion is Christianity, particularly the Baptist and Evangelical branches of the Christian faith.

Farm life

- Income can be unpredictable due to the volatility of weather, animal health, and world food prices.
- Farms can be very isolated, often situated a great distance from social centers and commercial conveniences (such as shops, airports, and train lines). This means that often agricultural areas consist of many small, close communities.

2 *In groups, summarize the profile of a typical American agricultural worker. Do you think it describes the caller in this unit?*

3 *How would you use your profile information to improve your service skills? Complete the table below.*

Customer profile		Agent service skills
Earnings are generally below average income.	▶	Be sensitive and pro active in finding cost-effective solutions.
	▶	

2 Customer expectations: "thinking outside the box"

- The customer in this call wants individualized service: to buy the medicine from the source before it was packaged. He gets increasingly frustrated because:
  - his request and the reason behind it are not acknowledged by the agent,
  - the agent is unwilling to escalate the call to a person with more authority,
  - the agent makes company policy more important than customer satisfaction.

- American customer service is focused on individualized, personal service in which the customer is always right. For example, it is not unusual for a store assistant to offer style advice, to watch your bags for you, or compliment your looks. This is the level of customer service that is expected – and generally provided – in the United States.

- In order to provide this kind of individualized customer service, you need to "think outside the box." Thinking outside the box means finding solutions for your customer that may fall outside your usual job description, but not outside the principles of the company you represent. Individualized service will make your customer feel that you are engaging with his/her specific concern.

 1 *Listen to the call again, and note down the moments that the customer asked for individualized service. Then work in groups and discuss the following questions:*

1. Did the agent do a good job? Why / Why not?
2. Did the agent understand that the customer wanted individualized service? Give evidence from the call.
3. Did the agent think outside the box? Give evidence from the call.

2 *Now you try thinking outside the box. Work in pairs. Write three more profile facts about the customer in the call. Then suggest agent service skills to deal with the customer.*

Customer profile		Agent service skills
Customer's situation is "real bad" in his own words. He is a farmer who has lost cows to a preventable illness.	▶	Express sympathy for the death of his cows. This livestock is the caller's financial livelihood.
	▶	
	▶	
	▶	

G Role-play

○ *Work in pairs. Read the scenario and your rolecard carefully. Then act out the role-play.*

Scenario
A customer is calling the customer service number of a well-known bargain center store, The Bargain Lot, to inquire about returning a television. The Bargain Lot is popular with low- to middle-income earners, who are always seeking good value. One of the benefits of shopping at The Bargain Lot is its excellent return policy. For purchased items to be returned, several criteria must be met. The agent must decide if the caller's purchase will be refunded.

ROLECARD I

Caller
You are a first-year university student. You consider yourself a bargain shopper and have recently purchased a television on sale from The Bargain Lot. The television worked fine for the first week, but then the color and sharpness of the picture began to fade. You are calling The Bargain Lot to find out what the return policy is. You still have the original receipt dated one week ago, and you still have the TV which you have placed back into the original packaging. However you have lost the remote control.

ROLECARD 2

The agent
You are being asked if it is possible to return a television that seems to be defective. Use the form below and find out the information from the customer; decide whether you will allow the television to be returned.

Requirements for returns:
 ◆ name and contact details of caller
 ◆ serial number of television
 ◆ caller must still have purchase receipt
 ◆ all components of television (remote, manuals, etc.) must be returned in original packaging
 ◆ make and model of television
 ◆ description of the problem
 ◆ television must have no signs of mishandling

The Bargain Lot

Caller's Details

Full name: _____

Address: _____

_____

Telephone: _____   Cell phone: _____

Email: _____   Fax: _____

Product Details

Product make: _____   Model number: _____

Serial number: _____

Description of problem: _____

Original receipt: YES / NO   All components: YES / NO   Signs of mishandling: YES / NO

H Self-evaluation

Tasks	Check	Comments (areas for self-improvement)
A The call Did you understand the purpose of the call and detailed information, with particular reference to the caller's emotions?	☐	
B Focus on language How confident are you with using the present continuous tense? How about the phrasal verbs? Do you feel like you could use *just* to better communicate with a caller?	☐	
C Soft skills Do you feel able to predict customer needs? Do you feel confident about giving the caller feedback when he/she talks?	☐	
D Pronunciation Are you confident using contracted forms?	☐	
E Read and explain Can you read, synthesize, and then clearly explain to someone what you have read?	☐	
F Intercultural matters Do you feel confident using factual information about American farming culture to improve your customer service skills? How about "thinking outside the box"?	☐	
G Role-play For this unit overall, what were your strengths and weaknesses?		

3 Explaining and giving instructions

What you will learn!
At the end of this unit, you will have covered:

A The call: listening to understand the overall purpose and details of the call, as well as the feelings of the caller

B Focus on language: zero conditional ◆ giving instructions using imperatives and softeners ◆ some common American idioms

C Soft skills: giving clear instructions and explanations

D Pronunciation: connected speech

E Read and explain: reading and synthesizing information about a phone headset to explain to a customer in non-technical English

F Intercultural matters: cultural stereotypes ◆ understanding cultural differences in public and private information ◆ gathering private information

G Role-play: simulating a call center transaction about setting up an internet connection

A The call

1 Pre-listening activity

The caller says "I don't want people to have my phone details."
What do you think the call will be about?

2 Global listening activity

Note down how you think the caller and the agent are feeling throughout the call.
Think of two words to describe their feelings.

3 Detailed listening activity

Listen to the call again and put the following instructions from the dialog into the correct sequence.
Compare your answers with your partner/group.

☐	Say something like "Congratulations."	☐	Enter your new number.
☐	Tap on the MS ID field.	☐	Type in the number 1314.
☐	Enter your old number.	☐	Leave the phone for four hours.
☐	Type in the number 33.	☐	Type in another hash key.
☐	Tap the hash key twice.	☐	Press the space dialog box.

B Focus on language

1 Zero conditional

The zero conditional is used in English to describe facts or habits:
*If he **goes** shopping, he always **spends** too much.*
*If you **plug** it in when the battery is already charged, it **is** not good for the phone.*

1 *Look at the transcript and find as many zero conditionals as you can, and note down how they are used.*

Example of zero conditional	How it is used
Or if you want to override that caller-ID block, you just press 428 and then the number.	

2 Giving instructions using imperatives and softeners

There are many ways of giving instructions in English. Using imperatives is a common way to tell people what to do. Imperatives are formed by using the basic form of verb:
***Give** me a couple of minutes.*
***Leave** the phone for four hours.*

Using one imperative after another is common when you have several steps in the procedure:
***Say** something, then **tap** OK.*

1 *Sit back-to-back with a partner. Give clear step-by-step instructions for one of the actions below. Your partner will write the instructions down while you are speaking. Swap roles and repeat with a different action.*

- Tie a shoe lace
- Make a cup of tea
- Brush your teeth

Instructions can be softened by using forms such as:
I want you to do X. / I'd like you to do Y. / I need you to do Z.

These can be used when you are starting the process, or you hit a problem in the process and the listener is having difficulty with the instructions. Intonation and sentence stress are also very important when giving instructions.

 2 *Note down some examples of the forms the agent uses to soften his instructions:*
I need you to tap the hash key twice.

3 Using idioms

1 *Look at the following idioms you hear in call centers. Match them with their meaning.*

Idiom	Meaning
1. The IT engineer is **troubleshooting** that problem right now.	a) to try again
2. **You're breaking up**. Can I call you back?	b) warning or prediction
3. The computer **is down** again.	c) finding out and fixing
4. I'm giving you a **heads up** on this.	d) I can't hear you clearly.
5. Let's **give it another try**.	e) to take over responsibility
6. He'll **pick it up** from here.	f) to inspect
7. We'll **get back on track** with this on Monday.	g) Finally I paid.
8. I **ended up paying** for it.	h) your responsibility
9. It's **down to you** to fix it.	i) to resume the work
10. I'll **take a look** at it.	j) has crashed

2 *Perform a call center scene using idioms correctly and in context.*

Instructions
Your trainer will scatter idioms on pieces of paper on the floor. Two students get up in front of the class and improvise a call center exchange based on the scenario below. The trainer gives a signal and students take turns picking up an idiom from the floor. They have ten seconds to find a way to use the idiom so that it makes sense. Otherwise they are out! Each time someone goes out, another student replaces him/her.

Scenario
A young woman had called to say that the wrong food basket has been delivered to her sister, who is a vegetarian. She asked for cheeses and dried fruit, and the basket contained canned ham and duck pâté. The young woman is also complaining because she ordered the Superior Basket and she has been charged for the Deluxe Basket.

C Soft skills

1 Giving clear instructions and explanations

> Giving instructions and explanations over the phone can be difficult because you cannot see what the other person is doing, or what he/she has already done. In this unit, you heard an example of how to give instructions. You will be learning how to do the same with your own customers.
>
> The rules for giving clear instructions and explanations:
>
> 1. Keep the language simple: don't use unnecessary jargon or idioms.
> 2. Start with a summary statement. For example: *I'm going to tell you about the new features of your cell phone.*
> 3. Start each point with the main topic, and then expand. For example: *The new ring-tone menu is an excellent feature. You are now able to choose from your ten favorite pop tunes.*
> 4. Check understanding with the caller as you go along.
> 5. Summarize at the end and check for understanding. For example: *OK, so that's the new features of your phone. Does that all make sense to you?*
> 6. Remember your listener! You may need to modify your explanations and instructions for your audience. For example, the caller may be a non-expert speaker or an older person who has difficulty hearing.

1 *In small groups, listen to the call and read the transcript again. Find as many examples of the six rules for giving clear instructions and explanations as you can.*

2 *Work in pairs. Your trainer will give you both a picture. Take turns describing your picture to your partner, using the rules above, while your partner tries to draw the picture based on your instructions. (Make sure your partner doesn't see the picture!) Compare your drawing with the original picture.*

3 *Discuss with the class the last task:*

- Was it easy or difficult?
- Was the end result similar to the original picture?
- Why do you think it worked / didn't work?
- How could you improve if you did this activity again?

4 *Work in pairs. Student A explains how to get from his/her home to work. Student B is a non-expert speaker whose English is limited. Student A should give a clear explanation.*

5 *In the same pairs, Student B instructs Student A how to use the text messaging function on a cell phone. Student A is an elderly person who is slightly deaf and has never used a cell phone before.*

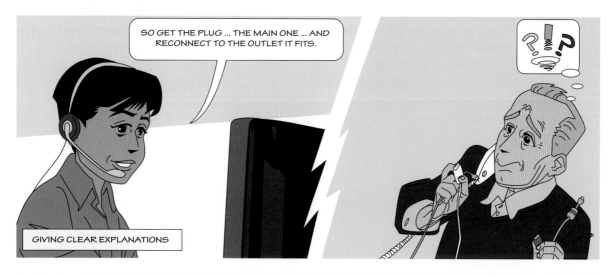

D Pronunciation

1 Connected speech

An important feature of natural speech is linking words together ("connected speech"). This has the effect of making two words sound like one word. There are three principles of connected speech to be aware of:

1. When a word ends with a consonant sound *(man)*, it links to the next word if it begins with a vowel sound *(arrived)*:

   The man arrived.

2. When a word ends with a vowel sound and the next word begins with a vowel sound, a /w/ or /y/ sound is added:

   He went through a tunnel. /w/
   Do all of you know what to do? /w/
   I can't really see it. /y/
   My uncle is home. /y/

3. When a word ends with a certain consonant sound and the next word begins with the same or similar consonant sound, the shared sound is longer and connects the two words:

   I'll go next time.
   It was a tough fight.
   We saw some red deer.

 1 *Listen again to lines 1-35 of the call. Find one example of each principle above.*

 2 *Now listen to Additional Listening and note down five examples of each principle of connected speech that you hear.*

3 *Work with a partner. Using the examples of connected speech below, role-play a call center transaction. Then give each other feedback on pronunciation.*

1. They are late for an important meeting.
2. The new account number is six one nine, three eight eight, eight two one.
3. May I also have the name on the account?
4. I'll look at it now, sir.
5. May I get your phone number please with the area code first?

4 *In small groups, read aloud the sentences below and underline the points where words will be linked.*

1. I'm afraid I don't have that information at the moment.
2. Could you allow us to make three installments?
3. It isn't an acceptable form of payment.
4. We aren't interested in opening up a new policy.
5. To open an account, you apply online.

5 *Work in pairs. Sit back-to-back. Student A reads the sentences below to Student B. Student B writes down which words he/she heard connected. Switch roles and repeat. Compare what you have written down. Read as quickly and naturally as possible.*

1. Can I ask you if there are any penalties?
2. Please clear up your overdue account as soon as possible.
3. Should I apply even if I don't have a spouse?
4. I don't want anyone else to know I have activated it.
5. We are in a rural area, so it won't apply to us.

E Read and explain

○ *Spend one minute skimming the text below, and then complete the paired activity.*

How to use your Airhead headset

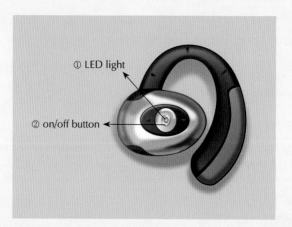

① LED light

② on/off button

1. Make sure the battery is charged

Keep an eye on the battery and make sure it is fully charged. When you use your Airhead for the first time, you will need to charge it for 12 hours.

2. How to turn your Airhead on

When your Airhead is turned off, press and hold down the on/off button for 3 seconds to turn it on – this will power up your Airhead. You'll know it is on when you hear a constant high tone and the LED light turns red for 3 seconds. This then turns to an intermittent green flashing and the high tone disappears. You are ready to use your Airhead.

3. How to turn your Airhead off

When your Airhead is on, press and hold down the on/off button for 6 seconds to turn it off. You'll know it is off when you hear a constant high tone and the LED turns red for 3 seconds. This then turns black and the high tone disappears. You are ready to put your Airhead away.

4. How to put your Airhead in pairing mode

Pairing is when your headset and your cell phone are connected up and responding to each other. Make sure that your charging cable is not connected to your Airhead before you start pairing.

You'll know your phone is in pairing mode after you have held down the on/off button for 4 seconds and it flashes alternately red and green.

Then go to the menu on your phone and select the connection "pair" from your menu. Your Airhead will flash green every 3 seconds when you have successfully selected the pairing mode. If you have difficulty setting up this function, turn off the headset and repeat all the steps.

---

1 *Role-play these situations in pairs. Swap roles for the second task.*

1. **Caller:** I've just received an Airhead cell phone set for my birthday, but I can't understand what I need to do to "pair" it. Can you explain?

    Agent: *Use the information in the text and explain in your own words without reading directly from the text.*

2. **Caller:** Help! I don't know how to turn this headset off!

    Agent: *Use the information in the text to help the caller without reading directly from the text.*

F Intercultural matters

1 Cultural differences

▥ Problems with Western customers are due 90% of time to cultural differences rather than grammar or vocabulary errors. This means that as a call center agent you need to be aware of the cultural expectations and beliefs behind the language you use, and the language your customer uses. This is very important for your development as a culturally intelligent and flexible agent.

▥ To be flexible and aware of how culture affects a call, create a "profile" of your caller based on:

	Example
1. Knowledge of cultural norms	*In the United States, approximately 40% of marriages end in divorce.*
2. Facts about the caller	*The caller is a young woman from the North East.*
3. Observations or educated guesses about the caller	*The caller has crying children in the background. She mentions that she has two jobs.*

▥ Using these three points, a culturally intelligent agent can help the caller to complete the inquiry fast and efficiently. This caller is clearly pressed for time, and may not have anyone available to help with the children. The agent can also be proactive in finding cheaper solutions, since the caller has two jobs, which suggests that the household income is low.

2 Stereotypes

▥ Stereotypes are a way of grouping people by typical actions, attitudes, and personalities. These can be problematic if you see everybody as a stereotype. However, if you use them carefully and flexibly, generalizations can be useful.

1 *Work in groups. Select the words in the box that could be a generalization about your culture, American culture, and one other culture you know.*

funny	honest	shy	direct	aggressive
serious	considerate	diplomatic	reliable	authoritarian
organized	impatient	friendly	old-fashioned	egalitarian (equal)
creative	angry	individualistic	reserved	
emotional	open	self-righteous	respectful	

Your culture	American culture	One other culture

2 *In your groups, discuss the following questions and report your answers to the class.*

1. In your opinion, are there any similarities between your culture and American culture?
2. What are the key differences?
3. How accurate do you think these stereotypes are?
4. How helpful do think these stereotypes are?
5. How can understanding differences and similarities between your culture and American culture help you?

3 *Listen to the call again and look at the words you chose in Activity 1. Which words apply to this caller? Use evidence from the call to support your answers.*

Words describing the caller	Evidence from the call

3 Public and private information

By the term "public" we mean the kind of information that would be discussed by acquaintances (a group, for example, who have known each other for a week or two). By the term "private" we mean the kind of information that would only be discussed with family or close friends, or not discussed at all.

1 *Which of the subjects below do you consider public? Which are private? Underline those that you think Americans consider private. Compare your notes with a partner.*

salary	job	religion	weight	cost of items owned
children	weather	symptoms of illness	emotional state	political beliefs
current affairs	marital status	hobbies	age	sexual preference

4 Gathering private information

As a call center agent, you may be required to gather information that is considered private or semi-private by your American callers. In order to do this without upsetting a caller, you will need to observe some social rules for gathering private data:

Acknowledge: When you make the request for private information, acknowledge that the information is sensitive by saying something like *Forgive me for asking but …* , *I'm afraid that we will need to …* , or *Excuse me for asking but …* This lets customers know that you are aware of their position and are considering their feelings.

Be professional: Generally you will use a conversational and friendly tone for an interaction in order to build rapport, but when you gather private data your tone must be formal and detached, as if you are not personally interested in the information.

Don't comment: When gathering private information about a person, don't make conversational comments (such as *Wow! Your voice sounds younger than that!* or *That's a good salary for someone of your age!*). This is unlikely to put customers at ease, and will probably make them feel that you are taking an undue personal interest in their private data.

Explain why: When you ask for private information, always give the reason. For example, if you need to know the caller's age to confirm their identity, rather than asking *How old are you?* say *Could you provide your date of birth for verification purposes?*

1 *Ask for the following information from an American customer, using the rules given on the last page.*

1. You are an agent for a health line. You need to take detailed information about the caller's health complaint (such as symptoms) before passing him/her on to a specialist. This information will help you to screen out prank callers and decide which specialist to transfer the caller to.

2. You are an agent for a loans company. You need to gather information on the caller's salary, home life (marital status, children), and history of health in order to decide whether the loan application is worth passing on to a superior. Your performance is measured by how many good applications you pass on, so you must gather detailed information in order to screen out hopeless candidates.

G Role-play

○ *Work in pairs. Read the scenario and your rolecard carefully, and act out the role-play.*

Scenario

A university student has recently purchased a new laptop for writing assignments and research. The internet needs to be connected so that the resources on the web can be accessible to the student. For this to happen, a new account must be created, and the caller must follow instructions to set up the connection.

ROLECARD I

Caller

You are a young, demanding, and time-conscious university student. You want services to be done efficiently and quickly. You are calling an internet service provider to set up the internet. You want a fast internet connection so you can research and find sources for your assignments. Find out what the requirements are and request that it be done today.

ROLECARD 2

Agent

A student needs to set up an internet connection. You must first set up an account and then provide some instructions to set up the connection. Payment must be secured from the caller before setting up the internet connection. Make sure you gather the caller's name, address, contact telephone number, and payment option. Below are the options available to the student.

INTERNET CONNECTION OPTIONS

	Modem connection (slow)	DSL connection (fast)
Price	US$12.00/month	US$27.00/month
Connection activation time	Very fast, can be done over the phone because it will use modem and regular telephone line.	Will require a technician to come and install a new modem. 3–4 business days.
Payment	credit card / direct debit	credit card / direct debit
Set-up steps	1. Make sure modem is enabled / turned on. 2. Plug telephone cord into modem. 3. In control panel, right click on modem and select "Properties." 4. Enter 410-345-1234 in phone number box. 5. Press "Save" settings. 6. Right click on modem again and select "Connect to internet." 7. Modem will make connection sounds, after which, open your web browser and you will be able to surf the web.	Technician will set up connection.

H Self-evaluation

Tasks	Check	Comments (areas for self-improvement)
A The call Did you understand the purpose of the call and the detailed information, with particular reference to the caller's emotions?	☐	_____
B Focus on language Are you confident about giving instructions? Do you understand how to use the zero conditional? How about the meanings of some common American idioms?	☐	_____
C Soft skills Are you comfortable giving instructions and explanations to a customer?	☐	_____
D Pronunciation Can you correctly use connected speech?	☐	_____
E Read and explain Can you read, synthesize, and then clearly explain to someone what you have read?	☐	_____
F Intercultural matters Do you understand the importance of being aware of cultural differences? Can you use stereotypes effectively and open-mindedly? Do you feel confident requesting private information which is culturally sensitive?	☐	_____
G Role-play For this unit overall, what were your strengths and weaknesses?		_____

4 Defusing anger

What you will learn!

At the end of this unit, you will have covered:

A The call: listening to understand the overall purpose and details of the call, as well as the feelings of the caller

B Focus on language: modal verbs used for making assumptions ◆ more phrasal verbs

C Soft skills: defusing anger ◆ sounding sincere

D Pronunciation: understanding and using intonation to express emotions

E Read and explain: reading and summarizing credit card information to explain to a customer in non-technical English

F Intercultural matters: money matters in American culture ◆ accepting responsibility, understanding blame and accountability in customer expectations

G Role-play: simulating a call center transaction about bank fees

DAN and DORA. AN ANGRY CUSTOMER

⊠$ %!!?**$ $ π˙ßåʃ√?!!!**æ˙©∂∑˙*!!!

SHE WANTS TO TALK TO YOU.

OK, I'LL DEFUSE. IT'S A DIFFICULT BUT ESSENTIAL SKILL.

LIKE DEFUSING A BOMB?

A The call

1 Pre-listening activity

The caller says "There was $15 but you're not able to explain it to me."
What do you think the call will be about?

2 Global listening activity

🔘 *Listen to the call. Rank how well this call was handled by the agent on a scale of 1 to 10 (the highest is 10). Explain your choice.*

3 Detailed listening activity

🔘 *Look at the list of adjectives below and note whether you think they relate to the caller (C) or the agent (A) or neither (N). Work in pairs. Explain your selections.*

☐ efficient	☐ distracted
☐ irate	☐ robotic
☐ patient	☐ bemused
☐ friendly	☐ helpful
☐ rude	☐ frustrated
☐ proactive	☐ worried
☐ indifferent	☐ reactive
☐ unhelpful	☐ professional

B Focus on language

1 Modal verbs

> ▥ Modal verbs express possibility, intention, obligation, logical deduction, and assumptions about a situation:
> *He **must** be an experienced call center agent. (necessity/logical deduction)*
>
> ▥ Many modal verbs can have more than one function:
> *You **should** do that. (obligation/necessity/advice)*
> *I **must** go to the bank. (intention/obligation/necessity)*
>
> ▥ Assumptions about the past can be expressed with a modal verb + *have* + past participle:
> *I can't find my car keys. I **might/could/may** have left them in the car last night.*

1 *Give examples of modals that express the functions listed below. Remember, some modals have more than one function. Think of sentences containing the modal verbs and discuss them in pairs.*

Function	Modal verb(s)
obligation	*must, should*
possibility/probability	
permission	
logical deduction	
necessity	
polite offer/request	
ability	

2 *Look for modals in the transcript and decide which function they have.*

3 *Respond to the prompts below using modals of assumption in the present.*

1. You can't find your car keys.
    They must still be in the car.
2. Your friend is late for a lunch appointment.
3. Your plane is still on the runway after one hour.
4. The computer won't start.
5. This meal tastes odd.
6. Your mother isn't answering her phone.
7. The flowers in the office are dying.

4 *Respond to the prompts below using modals to make assumptions about the past.*

1. Last night you lost $100 when you were out.
2. Yesterday your best friend sounded very upset on the phone.
3. Your sister was late getting home from the party last night.
4. Your workplace has just increased everyone's pay by 25%.
5. All the chocolates disappeared from the refrigerator yesterday afternoon.
6. Your colleague has just been promoted.
7. The book your friend borrowed two months ago still hasn't been returned.

2 Phrasal verbs (2)

Some phrasal verbs can be separated when they have an object:
*I'm going to **give** this job **up**.* → *I'm going to **give it up**.*

You can also say I'm going to **give up** this job, but not I'm going to give up it.

1 *Complete the table below. Check that you know the meaning of the phrasal verb first.*

Sentences with phrasal verbs	Can the verb and particle be separated? If so, rewrite the sentence.
1. I'll bring up the matter with my supervisor.	
2. Can you drop off the letter on your way home?	
3. Can you look after my cats while I'm away?	
4. I'll look up the address on the web.	
5. He'll look into the matter tomorrow.	
6. I'll work out the exact amount I owe you when I get home later.	
7. Please put up my mother for a few days when she arrives.	

C Soft skills

1 Defusing anger

When callers are angry or frustrated, they may ask to speak to your supervisor. This can be upsetting because it sends out the message that the caller does not think you are capable of helping him/her. However, it is your job to avoid escalation by developing your skills in defusing anger and frustration, and working with the customer to solve the problem.

Key methods for defusing anger in American customers are:

- **Acknowledge:** Be sympathetic to the customer's concern by using phrases such as: *I can understand your frustration* or *Yes, this situation is unacceptable.*
- **Be confident:** Follow up acknowledgment with an assurance that you are committed to resolving the issue: *I can understand your frustration, but I'm here now to help, so let me look into this for you.*
- **Listen:** Make sure you have listened to the customer's complaint, even if it is tempting to hold the phone away from your ear! Don't interrupt when the customer is explaining the problem, but respond with acknowledgment and active confidence once he/she has finished.

The agent said: *I'm not able to provide you with why there was an excess 15-dollar fee* (line 72). A better response would be: *I see a 15-dollar fee and the **Collections** Department are the **best** people to **explain** to you why it occurred.* By stressing the content words *collections*, *best*, and *explain*, the agent shows confidence in solving the problem.

Some functional language to help you express listening, acknowledgment, and confidence:

I would be very frustrated as well if my credit card had been declined. I'm notifying the appropriate department as we speak.

I'm sorry, my supervisor is not available, but let me assure you that I can resolve the situation right now.

I'm sorry that no one got back to you, but if you can give me your policy number, I'll fast track your concern and handle it personally from here.

1 *Look at the transcript and highlight where the caller gets frustrated and asks to speak to the supervisor.*

2 *Divide into groups of three. Student A is the caller, Student B is the agent, Student C is a quality assurance person. Students A and B perform the scenarios below. Student C uses the Quality Assurance Feedback Form on the next page to give feedback to Student B on his/her defusing anger skills.*

Scenario 1
The caller wants to know about interest charges on a loan. Caller thinks that the company is overcharging him/her because the interest just went up.
The agent wants to explain that interest charges are variable, which is why interest fees are higher in certain periods of the year.

Scenario 2
The caller has been transferred eight times because he/she is unhappy with the customer service and has requested to speak to someone new. Caller's original problem was to report a stolen credit card and request that the company freeze the account. This is a simple process, but now he/she wants to speak to a supervisor to complain about the bad service received.
The agent: Your supervisor wants you to calm the caller down and deal with original inquiry without escalating the call.

Quality Assurance Feedback Form

Scoring System:
1 = Excellent (defused anger and made customer happy with service)
2 = Good (defused anger quickly and efficiently)
3 = Average (defused anger after some time)
4 = Poor (did not defuse anger)
5 = Unacceptable (increased anger!)

Defusing anger skills	Score	Comments
Listening to the customer		
Acknowledging anger		
Confidence in proactively solving the problem		
Did the call end with the issue resolved?		

2 Sounding sincere

■ The agent in this call seems to be "going through the motions." In other words, at times the agent's responses sound mechanical. You need to be aware of your intonation and how sincere you are sounding. Whether you are greeting, thanking, apologizing, or explaining, you must sound sincere.

■ Sincerity will make your customer feel cared for, and could help defuse anger. Boredom (or a "robotic" voice) will make your customer feel that he/she doesn't matter, and could increase anger.

■ In line 98 of the transcript the agent thanks the caller for holding by saying: *Is there anything else I can assist you with?* The phrase is said in a monotone, and sounds insincere. In order to sound sincere, the agent should have stressed the words *else* and *assist* with a rising intonation and the final word, *with*, should have been spoken with rising intonation:
*Is there anything **else** I can **assist** you **with**?*

You will learn more about rising intonation in the next section of this unit.

 1 *Listen to the call and note down where you think the agent sounded mechanical. Write down an improved version, underlining the stressed words. Then practice your improved responses with a partner.*

2 *Work in pairs. Student A reads aloud caller quotes 1 to 3. Student B responds in the sincerest manner possible. Then swap roles. Student B reads caller quotes 4 to 6 and Student A responds.*

1. You didn't explain this application form properly!
2. I'm having trouble installing this program onto my computer. Why aren't your instructions clearer?
3. What do you mean you can't give me that information?
4. That stupid phone you sent me isn't working!
5. How dare you charge so much for interest?
6. Do you take me for an idiot? I'm not paying for a service that I'm not happy with!

D Pronunciation

1 Understanding and using intonation to express emotions

▦ Emotion is shown more by intonation (voice tone) than the actual words you use. If you say *I've had a **great** time* using an excited tone, the message you send out is very different than if you say it in a bored tone.

▦ A good call center agent should be able to not only detect emotion through the caller's voice, but also communicate appropriate emotions through his/her own voice.

▦ It is important to remember that word stress can also affect how we express emotion. The same words can communicate very different meanings through intonation and word stress combined.

 ♦ *What is your **name** again?*

If the word *name* is stressed with falling intonation at the end, the speaker sounds angry or frustrated.

 ♦ *What is your name **again**?*

If the word *again* is stressed with raising intonation at the end, the speaker sounds like he/she is politely requesting.

▦ Sarcasm and appreciation: although the difference between being polite and being angry is usually very clear, there are some emotions that are harder to distinguish. For example, the difference between sarcasm and appreciation:

Thank you. You've been very helpful. (= You have solved my problem. OR You haven't helped me at all!)

 1 *Work in pairs. Look at the transcript of the call and underline where you think the caller is expressing frustration or anger. Then listen and check your answers.*

 2 *In the same pairs, say aloud the phrases that you identified in the last activity, but use a different intonation. Your partner writes down what feelings you communicated.*

 3 *Listen to Additional Listening with the sentences below.*
 Do they show sarcasm (S) or appreciation (A)?

> 1. You've been very helpful. .... ☐
>
> 2. The instructions were really clear. .... ☐
>
> 3. Thank you for your time and effort. .... ☐
>
> 4. I'm thrilled that this was done the way it was. .... ☐
>
> 5. I appreciate you letting me know so soon. .... ☐
>
> 6. Are all of your agents as knowledgeable as you are? .... ☐

 4 *Work in pairs. Look at the following sentences. Write two short dialogs which include them. In the first dialog, the caller is angry or sarcastic. In the second, the caller is politely requesting. Role-play the calls using the right intonation.*

 1. Do you know the reason for this?
 2. Nobody told me. Could you explain it?
 3. Would you mind checking again?

E Read and explain

○ *Spend one minute skimming the text, and then complete the paired activity on page 42.*

Canceling the Axe Credit Card

Find out why!

The caller may have many reasons for canceling his/her credit card, and it is good to work this out before you instruct him/her how to cancel the card. You may be able to convince the customer to retain the card. The reasons may include:

- general dissatisfaction with the credit card service.
- extra and increased charges.
- lack of self-discipline in spending.

Reasons not to cancel ...

1. It's a good line of credit.
Ask if the customer is expecting to buy a large item, e.g. a car, in the near future. Explain that having qualified for a loan, the credit card provides a good line of credit.

2. It may affect your credit rating!
Also, if the customer closes his/her account, the credit rating may be negatively affected.

Credit scoring models may include the result of our "Axe Credit Formula." The Axe formula results in a fraction of less than one. THE LOWER THE FRACTION, THE BETTER!

Here is an example: If you have a debt of $1,000 and you have available credit of $10,000, your Axe score will be 0.1. This is because you are only using one-tenth of the credit available to you. However if you have a debt of $9,000, and you have $10,000 available credit, your Axe score will be 0.9. The closer your fraction is to 1.0, the more it hurts your credit!

3. If you still have an outstanding balance ...
We have a legal right to raise your interest rate to the maximum allowable by law if you are canceling your card and you still owe money.

Advise the customer to get rid of any outstanding balance on his/her credit card before canceling the card!

Procedure ...

1. Notify us. Phone and talk to a customer service representative.

2. Must notify in writing, providing name, address, and contact details.

3. Fill in the Can39289 form and send by email, fax, or mail.

4. Check that credit balance is correct on the latest statement.

5. Cut up your old card so no one else can use it!

1 *Role-play these situations in pairs. Swap roles for the second task.*

1. **Caller:** I've just about exceeded the credit on my card and I'm really worried. I think I should just cancel the card.

   Agent: Explain clearly why this may not be a good idea as far as his/her credit rating may be concerned, without reading directly from the text.

2. **Caller:** OK, now that I've informed you by phone that I want to cancel my credit card, what else do I need to do?

   Agent: Try and find out the reason for cancellation and then explain clearly what the procedure is, without reading directly from the text.

F Intercultural matters

1 Money matters in American culture

AVERAGE INCOME
Median income levels range from approximately US$40,000 a year to around US$65,000 a year.

LOW-INCOME STATES ARE:
Mississippi, Arkansas, Louisiana.

MID-INCOME STATES ARE:
Georgia, New York, Wisconsin.

HIGH-INCOME STATES ARE:
New Jersey, Maryland, New Hampshire.

Major Expenses, by Income Levels
Percent saying this is a major expense

| | All Adults | Family Income | | | |
		Under $30K	$30K-$49K	$50K-$99K	$100K & over
	%	%	%	%	%
Medical or dental bills	45	58	49	36	32
Clothing	34	41	34	28	36
Eating at restaurants	34	24	34	40	48
Vacation travel	29	20	22	34	49
Entertain friends & family	23	19	23	22	32
Home furnishings	17	21	16	15	23
Jewelry	7	8	6	5	8

Pew Research Center

WHAT YOUR INCOME BUYS YOU
A global magazine originated the idea of understanding the cost of living by comparing the prices of McDonald's Big Macs across the globe. We are going to take this further and give some other typical prices so that you can get a sense of what the value of the dollar is for an average American:

Movie ticket:	*US$11*
Big Mac:	*US$3.50*
Pair of jeans:	*US$38*
Cappuccino:	*US$3*
Rent of mid-range apartment:	*US$1,500 per month*

CREDIT CARDS
Credit card usage is very high in the United States. Cards (credit or debit) are used in preference to cash. The average American has four credit cards, and has access to approximately US$19,000. Up to 14% of Americans carry ten credit cards or more.

There are 1,488,000,000 credit cards in usage in the United States, which means there are five times as many credit cards as there are people.

1 *Look at the information on the previous page. Prepare five-minute presentations about the differences and similarities between American attitudes and habits concerning money and those of your own culture.*

2 *Work in pairs. Select four facts from the text and use your cultural intelligence to think of ways to improve your service skills.*

American culture information		Service skills
Cards are used in preference to cash by most Americans.	➡	If one is lost, this is likely to be very upsetting. A good agent will be sympathetic and proactive in finding a fast solution, since cards are used on a daily basis.
	➡	

2 Taking responsibility and understanding blame and accountability

▤ The cause of frustration in this call was not the amount of money that had been deducted (US$15). The customer was angry that the agent was not able to explain *why* the amount had been deducted.

▤ An important part of American service culture is direct and open communication. This will help you to gain the trust and respect of your American caller. Unfortunately, in order to appear competent, many agents will not admit that they don't know the answer to a question, and prefer to guess at an answer (as the agent did in this call).

▤ The caller lets the agent know that he thinks he has been treated badly and that something has gone wrong by saying: *I'm trying to be patient myself here, you know, be courteous, all of that … It just seems like strange customer service from the company.* The agent's response to this does not take responsibility or acknowledge the problem. She says: *Sure. OK. Anyway, I'll be transferring your call now.*

▤ If your caller thinks you are trying to cover up a problem, or that you are pretending to understand something that you don't, he/she is likely to feel that you are not trustworthy. He/She may even ask for a supervisor (as the caller in this call did) because he/she does not trust the information or reasons you are giving. Your job is to keep the trust of your callers by maintaining their confidence that you can help them.

1 *Look at the transcript and note down the strategies the agent uses to appear competent (even though she was not able to help the caller). Discuss why these strategies worked or didn't work. How could the agent have improved her strategies to defuse the anger?*

Strategy	Why did/didn't it work?	Improved strategy
Guessing at reasons for the US$15 deduction.		

2 *Work in pairs. Write responses for the following scenarios, taking into account what you have learned about American incomes, and being open and taking responsibility.*

1. Your caller has just lost her purse. This contains all seven of her credit cards. She has called to freeze her account, but you are not allowed to authorize this, so you will need to transfer her to another department.

2. Your caller has discovered that he was charged twice for one purchase. The total extra charge was US$40. He wants to contest the charge through you. You are able to register the customer contesting the charge. However the customer may not receive a refund because the payment has already been received and the company information is listed as private.

G Role-play

○ *Work in pairs. Read the scenario and your rolecard carefully, and act out the role-play.*

Scenario

An angry caller is calling the bank about a problem with his/her fees. The caller does not understand where these fees are coming from or what they are for. The caller demands to speak to a supervisor. Escalation policy requires agents to try every possible way of helping the customer before escalating to a supervisor. The agent must decide if this call is to be escalated or not. The supervisor will not take the call unless you complete the form below.

ROLECARD I

Caller

You are an extremely busy manager of a large corporation. You are angry that mysterious fees have appeared on your bank statement:

- The fees amount to US$30 in total.
- No details about the fees are provided; they are labeled miscellaneous.
- You refuse to speak to anyone but a supervisor or manager.
- If unable to speak to a manager, get more irate.
- Demand that this issue be dealt with at once.

ROLECARD 2

Agent

A very angry customer tells you that he/she will only talk to a supervisor. For you to be able to transfer the call to a supervisor you must:

- obtain the name of the caller.
- ask for the reason why the call needs to be handled by a supervisor.

The supervisor will not take the call unless you have these details.

Call Escalation Requirements		
Name of Caller:		
Contact Details:	Phone:	Email:
Reason for Escalation:		
Escalate:	❑ YES	❑ NO

H Self-evaluation

Tasks	Check	Comments (areas for self-improvement)
A The call Did you understand the purpose of the call and detailed information, with particular reference to the caller's emotions?	☐	
B Focus on language How do you feel about using modal verbs of assumption? Do you now understand how some modals can communicate more than one functional meaning depending on the context? How about phrasal verbs?	☐	
C Soft skills Do you feel more confident about defusing anger in customers, and sounding sincere?	☐	
D Pronunciation Do you feel you have understood the importance of intonation in expressing emotions?	☐	
E Read and explain Can you read, synthesize, and then tell someone what you have read?	☐	
F Intercultural matters Can you use your knowledge of American attitudes and habits regarding money to improve your service skills, and your understanding of cultural expectations to help you defuse anger?	☐	
G Role-play For this unit overall, what were your strengths and weaknesses?		

5 Probing for information and admitting mistakes

What you will learn!
At the end of this unit, you will have covered:

A The call: listening to understand the overall purpose and details of a call, as well as the feelings of the caller

B Focus on language: using the second conditional to give advice ◆ the interrupted past ◆ more common American idioms

C Soft skills: probing for information ◆ admitting mistakes

D Pronunciation: omitting consonants and syllables in natural speech

E Read and explain: reading and synthesizing information about cameras to explain to a customer in non-technical English

F Intercultural matters: higher education and family ties

G Role-play: simulating a call center transaction about a faulty MP3 player

DAN and DORA - DON'T ARGUE WITH A CALLER!

OK, TO DEFUSE, YOU'LL NEED TO APOLOGIZE AND TAKE RESPONSIBILITY FOR THE PROBLEM.

BUT IT'S NOT MY FAULT!

I'M REALLY SORRY THIS HAPPENED TO YOU, MA'AM. LET ME SEE HOW I CAN RECTIFY ...

A The call

1 Pre-listening activity

The agent says "I thought it was said here it was dropped. It wasn't."
What do you think the call will be about?

2 Global listening activity

 Listen to the call. Does the caller feel that his problem has been understood?
Note down the main advice given by the agent.

3 Detailed listening activity

 Listen to the call again and choose the best answers to the questions below.

1. The caller is calling because
    a) his camera is not working.
    b) he needs an authorization number.
    c) he wants to know if he should send in everything, such as the battery charger.
    d) he thinks he is using the wrong batteries.

2. The authorization number is
    a) 56783468.
    b) 56783648.
    c) 56788463.
    d) 56783488.

3. The agent says the caller needs to send
    a) only the camera.
    b) the camera and the charger.
    c) the camera and the battery.
    d) the camera and the memory card.

4. The agent thinks that the problem with the camera could be because
    a) it was dropped.
    b) the caller is using the wrong batteries.
    c) the charger is faulty.
    d) the battery compartment has alcohol in it.

5. The agent suggests that the caller should clean the battery compartment with
    a) cotton swabs.
    b) a wet cloth.
    c) a dry cloth.
    d) a liquid such as alcohol.

6. How does the caller feel at the end of the call?
    a) frustrated about the advice.
    b) confused about what to do next.
    c) clear about the next steps.
    d) pessimistic about getting the camera working again.

7. The best way to describe the agent in this call is
    a) friendly and informative.
    b) bossy and unclear.
    c) empathetic.
    d) unhelpful.

8. The reason the caller is not required to send in the accessories is that
    a) he is using the Snapshot charger.
    b) he has no accessories.
    c) the agent thinks the caller will fix the camera by cleaning it.
    d) none of the above.

B Focus on language

1 The interrupted past

▨ When the past simple tense and the past continuous tense are used together in the same sentence, it is sometimes called the "interrupted past":
I was explaining to the caller how to make the insurance claim, and the line went dead.
This news was not what I was hoping for.
The past continuous is formed with: *was/were* + verb+ *-ing*

▨ The past continuous can be used to explain or make excuses:
Supervisor: *Why were you late for work again today?*
Agent: *I'm really sorry, I **was helping** my grandmother take out the garbage and I missed my train.*

Caller: *This is the third time I've called to get that document sent out. What are you doing?*
Agent: *Oh, I'm sorry. I **was training** all last week and wasn't at work. I'll get it to you right away, Ms. Brown.*

1 *Why is the past continuous called the interrupted past? Discuss in pairs.*

2 *Use the interrupted past to complete the dialog.*

1. A: Why didn't you send the refund right away?

   B: *I was preparing the refund when the computer system crashed.* ....

2. A: Where were you when the purse went missing?

   B: ....

3. A: Why are you late for the meeting?

   B: ....

4. A: You promised the report by yesterday.

   B: ....

5. A: How did you manage to crash the car?

   B: ....

6. A: Did you burn the dinner again?

   B: ....

3 *Find examples of the past continuous in the transcript. Discuss with a partner why it is used in each of the examples you find. Was it used as an excuse? Was it simply to describe something in the past?*

2 The second conditional

▨ The second conditional is used to express something that is improbable or hypothetical, or to give advice:

if + *simple past (clause 1)*	would + *verb (clause 2)*

Note that sentences can also begin with clause 2.

▨ Look at the examples below:
* Improbable: *If I **won** a lot of money, I **would go** shopping in Tokyo.*
* Hypothetical: *If you **ate** ten packets of cookies a day, you **would put** on a lot of weight.*
* Giving advice: *If I **were** you, I **would try** being a bit more patient with the caller.*

Notice that the *if* part of the sentence contains a past simple, but it refers to something in the future.

▨ Sometimes *would* is misused by agents because they believe it sounds polite. For example: *I would do that for you* doesn't mean "I am making a commitment to do that for you." It sounds improbable rather than polite. The agent thinks he/she has reassured the customer, but the customer feels unsure whether the action will be action. In this case it would be better to say: *I will do that for you.*

1 *Use a second conditional to respond to the prompts. Note whether your response is* improbable, hypothetical, *or giving advice.*

1. **A:** I have an awful toothache!

   B: ....

2. **A:** Do you gamble your monthly salary on the horse races?

   B: ....

3. **A:** Can I drive your car into the city at top speed?

   B: ....

4. **A:** Would you like to win the lottery?

   B: ....

5. **A:** Can you do double shifts at work all next week?

   B: ....

6. **A:** I don't want to work hard, but I want to get into the best university.

   B: ....

3 American idioms (2)

1 *Discuss the meanings of these idioms. Then use them in your own mini dialogs.*

- ◆ head out
- ◆ tell somebody off
- ◆ What's up with it?
- ◆ has something to do with
- ◆ We're all set now?

2 *Give phrasal verb idioms for the definitions using the verbs below. Can you think of more idioms with the same verbs?*

send - head - set - turn

to lead a company or project	*head up*	to celebrate someone leaving	_____
warning	_____	to leave	_____
something that disgusts you	_____	to explain	_____
to go to bed	_____		

I CAN'T BELIEVE MARIA TURNED DOWN THE TEAM LEAD POSITION. SHE WOULD HAVE BEEN PERFECT FOR IT!.

DID YOU KNOW THAT THE PERSON THEY OFFERED IT TO ALWAYS TURNS UP LATE?

C Soft skills

1 Probing questions

- A probing question is a question you ask to gather more details. Probing for more information from the customer is an important skill to develop.

- Probing will enable you to ensure that you have all the details you need, and you understand the problem or situation completely.

- Some callers may not like to give all the details at first, particularly if the topic is sensitive or embarrassing. Effective probing skills will help you to gather this information while putting the customer at ease.

- Probing questions may not be full questions because you and the caller know the context. For example:

  So you would like to purchase a new cell phone? What types of functions would you like on your new cell phone? **Do you want texting? And a camera?**

  You mentioned you recently bought a computer. What was the exact date of the purchase? **Who was the supplier? And cost?**

  So you're having problems accessing your account online. Can you tell me what steps you took to log on? **Did you key in your password? And Social Security number?**

1 *Work in pairs. Look at the transcript of the call. Highlight where the agent uses probing questions.*

2 *In groups discuss these questions.*

1. Are there too many / too few probing questions? Why?
2. What did these questions do to help the agent to perform her job?
3. How did the probing questions affect the caller?

3 *Work in pairs. Student A is the agent, Student B is the caller. Student A must find out as much information as possible from Student B by using probing questions. Swap roles for Scenario 2.*

Scenario 1

The caller wants a replacement cell phone after only one month of use because part of the screen does not work and it occasionally shuts down during calls. Caller dropped the phone several times and is embarrassed by this fact.

The agent gets details about the cell phone make, color, and the reason for returning it by using probing questions. Decide whether the cell phone should be replaced free of charge.

Scenario 2

The caller wants to book a hotel room for two.
The agent finds out sleeping arrangements and the name of both guests.

2 Admitting mistakes

- Occasionally agents will make errors. These can range from mispronouncing a caller's name to giving the wrong information. With American customers it is important to admit when you are wrong or have made a mistake, and then move forward to repair any damage and address the caller's concern.

- In this call the agent thought that the caller had dropped the camera. The caller responded to this mistake defensively, after which the agent admitted the mistake and apologized.

- Be sure to sound sincere when you apologize. Then rectify the error right away:

Caller: I would like to create a new account but in euros this time.

Agent: OK, so you would like to create a new account for deposits in Europe?

Caller: No, what I want is a local account, but I want to keep the money in euros.

Agent: **I'm terribly sorry, I misunderstood what you said.** Yes, I can create the account and the currency will not be converted.

Caller: I'm calling again about an order I placed yesterday.

Agent: I see, and you want to know the status of the delivery?

Caller: No, as I said already, I called earlier and I would like to add to that order.

Agent: **Oh, right. I've just realized that there are some notes from your previous call. Apologies for that!** Which items would you like to add?

1 ***In pairs, use these situations to practice admitting mistakes, repairing damage, and offering solutions.***

1. **Agent:** You use the caller's first name.
   Caller: You want the agent to address you by your last name.

2. **Agent:** You mispronounce the caller's business name "Waychewski."
   Caller: Your business name is Wavchowski Inc.

3. **Agent:** You suggest that the caller should make payments on time – but you are looking at the wrong file!
   Caller: You have never made a late payment.

4. **Agent:** You tell the caller that you will send a form to 22B Baker Street.
   Caller: Your mailing address is 23B Baker Street.

D Pronunciation

1 Silent consonants

- It is common in English to omit consonant sounds in fluent speech. This generally occurs when one consonant is immediately followed by another:
  I don know wha happen to it. (= I don't know what happened to it.)

- Usually, we do not silence the consonants /d/ and /t/ when they come before a vowel sound:
  the battery compartment of the camera (/t/ is pronounced)

- In some cases, silent consonants are not used because they could confuse the listener. For example, the sound /h/ at the beginning of a main word is not silenced even if it comes after another consonant sound:
  *We went on vacation because our **h**ouse was haunted.*

- Silent consonants are never used when a word is stressed for meaning or emphasis:
  *She stayed at home. Where did **he** go last night?* (*He* is stressed, so the /h/ is pronounced.)

1 *In groups, read through the first 20 lines of the transcript and highlight the consonants that you predict will be silent when spoken. Listen and check your answers.*

2 *Work in pairs. Practice saying the phrases with the silent consonants you found.*

3 *Say these sentences aloud. Highlight the consonants that you think will be silent in natural speech.*

1. The meeting ran late this morning.
2. I haven't seen him since last week.
3. What is her husband doing at the office? He should be at home.
4. Can you hold just for a moment? I won't be long.
5. I think that he would become the most valuable employee.
6. Could you send that document to him today, please?
7. The hotel burned down last summer.
8. We have never spent our vacation near home.

 4 *Now listen to the sentences above in Additional Listening 1 spoken by an American caller. Check your predictions!*

2 Silent syllables

It is common in natural speech in standard English to silence an entire syllable in words that have three or more syllables. There are many examples of this in the call:

cam'ra for *camera*
def'nitely for *definitely*

 1 *Look at the words below and decide which syllable is silent. Practice saying them aloud with a partner. Then listen to the words spoken by an American speaker in Additional Listening 2.*

Word	Pronunciation
basically	*basic'ly*
vegetable	
worsening	
actually	
automatically	
separate	
primary	

2 *Which of these words from the transcript have a silent syllable?*

alcohol ◆ especially ◆ accessories ◆ memory ◆ authorization
◆ batteries ◆ actually ◆ recommend

3 *Work in pairs. Make five sentences using the words from Activities 1 and 2 and practice pronouncing them.*

E Read and explain

○ *Spend one minute skimming the text, and then complete the paired activities below.*

Cameras 'R' Us

is a store devoted to providing customers with the best information about all cameras on the market, so they can make an informed decision when they purchase. **Cameras 'R' Us** is not affiliated with any particular brand of camera.

The **Cameras 'R' Us** guide to choosing your first camera.

Choosing your first camera involves deciding what you want to photograph, for what purposes, and to what quality level you want to take photographs. Here are some handy guidelines to give our customers when making their first camera purchase:

1 **Keep it simple!** Many cameras on the market nowadays are fully automated. For example, it is advisable to get a built-in auto focus and a built-in flash. This will make your life a lot easier.

2 **If you are interested in photography** there may be some features that you want to be able to control manually, such as the shutter speed.

3 **Think carefully about the lens** you want to buy. Remember that investing in your lens rather than the body is most important. Sometimes, sales assistants will persuade you otherwise. Buy the best lens you can afford with the basic body that suits your needs.

4 **Don't buy features that are too complex.** Start simple and then you can move to more complex functions once you've mastered the basics. When you first get a camera, it's usually a good idea to just get one with basic controls, although if you are a serious photographer, you may want to get a camera with a range of manual features. This will help you to understand how the camera works.

5 **Be careful when you read reviews** of cameras as they are often written by the sponsors and cannot be completely trusted as unbiased assessments of cameras.

6 **If you want to take photographs for fun** and have good results without thinking too much about the technical process, an auto-everything camera may be your best choice.

7 **Think seriously about whether you want to buy a new or used camera.** New cameras are expensive and you may be better off investing in a secondhand camera.

8 **One of the biggest mistakes you can make** is buying a camera because of the brand. The mere possession of a brand camera will not guarantee *National Geographic* – quality results in your photographs.

9 **Make sure you get a warranty or guarantee on your camera.** This is a big purchase item and you want to make sure that it can be readily replaced if anything goes wrong with it.

10 **Purchase from your local shop.** This will mean you can readily go back to the shop to ask questions, or return the camera if it is not working properly.

1 *Role-play these situations in pairs. Swap roles for the second situation.*

1. **Caller:** I'm going to be in Hong Kong next month and I've just gotten interested in photography. Do you have any advice?
   Agent: *Give three pieces of advice. Explain in your own words without reading directly from the text.*

2. **Caller:** I want a camera. It's just to take pictures of my children on important occasions, like birthdays.
   Agent: *Give three pieces of advice in your own words.*

F Intercultural matters

1 Higher education

The caller mentioned that he wants to give the camera to his son who is visiting from college so that he can send pictures back. In this section we look at higher education and family ties in the United States.

1 *Work in pairs. Read this information on higher education and compare it with your own country.*

Higher education	United States	Your country
Percentages	80% of Americans graduate from high school. 64% of high school graduates go to college. 29% of Americans finish college.	
Home or away?	According to a survey of American college freshmen, 44% attend colleges further than 100 miles from their home.	
Length	Typically, a college degree takes four years to complete.	
Cost	The cost of college tuition starts at US$5,000 a year (for some state colleges) and can go up to US$30,000 a year (for private colleges). Living expenses are estimated at US$10,000 a year. This means that if you have three children and want the "best" education opportunities for them, you will need to save nearly half a million dollars.	
Education is the 'best start in life'.	American culture views good education as something that should be available to everyone. Good education is directly linked to higher-earning jobs and is therefore the "best start in life." Because of the pressure on parents to provide their children with this opportunity, many American families start saving for college as soon as (or even before) their children are born.	

2 *Turn back to Unit 4 page 42 and look at the information on incomes. Discuss in groups how hard it would be for the average American to put two children through a moderately expensive university.*

2 Family ties

- According to the U.S. Census Bureau, just over 44% of households consist of at least one parent and one child. 56% of households are adults living alone, or with friends or partners.

- Only 3% of households contain three generations (grandparent, parent, and child). And 6% of households contain other relatives or non-relative members.

- The nuclear family (two parents and two children) is considered to be the typical American family. According to surveys this is also considered to be the "ideal" by a majority of Americans.

- The U.S. Census Bureau reports that approximately 40% of marriages in the USA end in divorce.

1 *Approximately 44% of Americans who attend college move further than 100 miles from home. What do you think this fact says about American culture and family life? Discuss in pairs.*

2 *Work in groups. Use the information on education and family ties to brainstorm five values of high importance (core values) and five values of low importance (non-core values) for Americans. Which ones are shared with your culture? Present your ideas to the class.*

Core values	Shared or different?
1. *Funding good education for your children*	
2.	
3.	
4.	
5.	
6.	

Non-core values	Shared or different?
1. *Living in extended family households*	
2.	
3.	
4.	
5.	
6.	

3 *Read the transcript again and, in pairs, underline clues the caller gives about his lifestyle. Focus particularly on education, family ties, and finance. Then use these clues to suggest what agent service skills are needed to deal with this particular customer.*

Customer profile		Agent service skills needed
	➡	
	➡	

4 *Now use your customer profile notes in a call center exchange.*

1 **Caller:** I'll choose Repayment Option 2. You see, I'm putting aside 5% of my income to send the kids to college when they grow up.

    You: *Oh, yes, it's so expensive, isn't it? But we all do it to give our kids the best! I'm putting you down for Option 2 as we speak.* ....

2. **Caller:** I want to buy a present for my daughter – not too expensive, but fashionable. She's just about to go to college in New York. I've never even been there!

    You: ....

3. **Caller:** I need to change our car insurance. My mother-in-law got sick recently, so she's coming to live with us.

    You: ....

G Role-play

○ *Work in pairs. Read the scenario and your rolecard carefully, and act out the role-play.*

Scenario

Selby Electronics is recognized worldwide as a manufacturer of high-quality electronic equipment. Selby employees take the time and care to resolve the customers' problems. If a caller has an item that is defective, details about the customer and the item must be obtained before recommending repair or replacement. The agent completes a form and decides whether to replace or repair the item.

ROLECARD I

Caller

You are a young professional who loves listening to music wherever you go. You recently purchased a Selby MP3 player and have some problems.

1. You think it is defective because it only works for 20 minutes before it needs recharging.
2. You didn't get a manual when you purchased the product, so you want one sent.
3. If the item needs to be repaired, you want a replacement while repairs are ongoing. You can't live without your music player!

You did not mishandle the product in any way, and you are eager to get it to work. The warranty is still current, and you have the receipt and warranty card for it. You really want to get this fixed because you like to listen to your music all the time. You called yesterday, but haven't heard anything.

ROLECARD 2

Agent

You work for Selby Electronics. While looking at your notes about this issue, you see a note referring to the MP3 player possibly having gotten wet. Find out if the caller has allowed the item to get wet, which might be why it is not working properly. Ask questions about the product and its warranty information so that you may help the caller.

Selby Electronics Inc.

Required Information:

Customer's name: ....

Customer's address: ....

....

Customer's phone number: ....   Customer's fax number: ....

Customer's email: ....   Date of purchase: ....

Product model number: ....   Product serial number: ....

Warranty number: ....   Battery serial number: ....

Was battery fully charged before initial use? ....

Was battery charged with Selby or Selby-approved charger? ....

Was product registered with Selby? ....

H Self-evaluation

Tasks	Check	Comments (areas for self-improvement)
A The call Did you understand the purpose of the call and detailed information, with particular reference to the caller's emotions?	☐	_____ _____ _____
B Focus on language Are you comfortable using the second conditional to give advice? Do you understand the interrupted past? How about common American idioms?	☐	_____ _____ _____
C Soft skills Can you effectively probe for information? How about admitting mistakes?	☐	_____ _____
D Pronunciation Are you able to pronounce silent consonants and syllables naturally?	☐	_____ _____
E Read and explain Can you read, synthesize, and then tell someone what you have read?	☐	_____ _____
F Intercultural matters Do you understand American values on family and education? Can you use this information to give better service to callers?	☐	_____ _____
G Role-play For this unit overall, what were your strengths and weaknesses?		_____ _____

6 Dealing with complaints and checking information

What you will learn!
At the end of this unit, you will have covered:

A The call: listening to understand the overall purpose and details of the call, as well as the feelings of the caller

B Focus on language: using modals to express obligation ◆ passives ◆ phrasal verbs

C Soft skills: dealing with complaints and checking information

D Pronunciation: word stress

E Read and explain: reading and synthesizing information from a letter of complaint to explain to a customer in non-technical English

F Intercultural matters: humor

G Role-play: simulating a call center transaction about mobile internet fees

DAN and DORA. —— IN THE COACHING ROOM

I CAN'T BELIEVE THE CALLER COMPLAINED AFTERWARD! HE SAID I'D BEEN VERY HELPFUL!

DID YOU THINK THE CALL WAS SUCCESSFUL?

NOT REALLY. HE YELLED A LOT.

SO POSSIBLY THE CUSTOMER WAS BEING SARCASTIC WHEN HE SAID YOU WERE BEING HELPFUL.

COME ON, LET'S GO THROUGH THE CALL.

A The call

1 **Pre-listening activity**

The caller says "Just curious, 'cause they sure cost us."
What do you think the call will be about?

2 Global listening activity

Listen to the call and write down five adjectives that you think best describe the caller. Now rank them in order of how important they are to understanding the caller. Justify your choices to your partner.

3 Detailed listening activity

Listen to the call again and note down whether you think the following statements are true (T) or false (F).

The caller …

1. went over the 800 minutes on the two phones according to the agent. .... ☐
2. found out the information through the website. .... ☐
3. was being charged for receiving texts. .... ☐
4. thinks she and her husband are being charged for off-peak calls. .... ☐
5. uses the text function. .... ☐
6. has had the phone for two years. .... ☐
7. often goes over the time limit on phone calls. .... ☐
8. requests the text messages to be blocked only on her phone. .... ☐

B Focus on language

1 Modals used to express obligation

There are many types of modals of obligation. Look at the examples below:
*They are **supposed to** give us off-peak rates after 9 p.m.*
*We **need to** pay our credit card bill on time.*
*We **don't have to** go to work tomorrow as it's a public holiday.*
*I **must** try to wake up earlier in the mornings!*

Obligation can be "internal" or "external" and still be expressed using the same words. For example:
I should clean up my computer. (I think I should.)
I should clean up my computer. (The boss told us all to do it!)

1 *Complete the dialog with your choice of modal verbs of obligation. In some cases, more than one correct answer is possible.*

Caller: Yes, I'd like to complain about my new credit card access. I haven't got my pin number yet! I need my credit card!

Agent: Oh, I'm so sorry about that. .... use your credit card today? What time do you need access? I might be able to assist you in accessing your card over the phone.

Caller: Oh, that would be fantastic. Thanks so much. I .... pay some overdue bills or else my electricity will be shut off.

Agent: OK, well, you .... give me your Social Security number.

Caller: Oh, let me see. I .... try and remember it!

Agent: You .... give it to me right now, but call me back in five minutes.

Caller: .... call my husband. He has a good memory for those kinds of things!

Agent: Ok call me back in five minutes, and I .... other details like bank card details, phone numbers, birthdays, etc. I .... gather this information to be sure you are really who you say you are!

Caller: OK, fair enough. I'll talk to you in a few minutes. Oh, by the way, ... wait for 12 hours after activating the card, or can I use it right away?

Agent: No, you can use it immediately!

2 Passives

> ▦ In the call center environment, it is common for callers to use the pronoun *they* to talk about an external party they don't know, or because they are more interested in the action itself.
> ▦ The passive form can be used to complain about or discuss an external party:
> **I am being charged** *excess time on my phone.*

1 *Fill in the passive forms. Note that you may need to change the main verb.*

They	Passive form
They are charging me for excess time on my phone.	*I am being charged for excess time on my phone.*
They want me to pay twice!	
They told me they would send it to me yesterday.	
They informed me it was late.	
They need to send it to me immediately.	
They are saying I haven't paid my bill.	
They have not delivered what they promised.	

3 Phrasal verbs (3)

1 *Go through the transcript and complete the table below with phrasal verbs you find.*

Line	Verb	Preposition	Meaning
6	*went*	*over*	*exceed the limit*

C Soft skills

1 Active listening

You have already learned about backchanneling and probing skills in earlier units. These are part of a larger skill that we call *active listening*. Being a good active listener is an essential skill for a call center agent, especially when the customer is feeling anxious, frustrated, or angry.

Listening is an active process which requires input from both listener and speaker. Active listeners listen and respond to the content, the context, and the hidden meaning of the communication.

Tips for active listening

1. Give the caller your undivided attention. Concentrate and focus!
2. Put yourself in the caller's shoes.
3. Listen for feelings! Research suggests that words communicate only 10% of the whole message. Tone and non-verbal clues like silence, laughing, and sighing will help you to determine the meaning.
4. Acknowledge your callers (backchanneling). Respond frequently so they know you are listening attentively.

Rules for active listening

Rule 1: Acknowledge how the customer is feeling. This communicates to the customer that you have listened and understood his/her emotional state:

I understand how frustrated/angry/anxious you must be feeling.
That's too bad. I do know what that feels like.

Rule 2: Make sure you understand exactly what his/her point of concern is. Paraphrase or summarize the point of concern to check understanding:

If I understand you correctly, your credit card was sent to the wrong address again.
Am I right in understanding that your booking was made for the wrong time but the date is OK?

Rule 3: Take action. Clearly explain what your next steps will be in resolving the issue:

OK, this is what I am going to do …
What I suggest I do immediately is …

1 *Work in pairs. Read the "Tips for active listening" above. Then tell your partner about your best friend for one minute, while your partner actively listens. Then switch roles and repeat.*

2 *Use the "Rules for active listening" above and respond to the caller in the dialogs below.*

Rule 1

Caller: Yes, I was expecting a technician to come fix my washing machine today, but he never showed up. I had to take a day off work, and it was a big waste of time.

Agent: ....

Rule 2

Caller: Yes, I have a question about my credit card. There is a $39 administrative fee on there. What's that about?

Agent: ....

Rule 3

Caller: But I wasn't told about the fee when I signed up for the card!

Agent: ....

3 *Read lines 3-10 of the transcript where the caller is explaining the problem. Write an improved agent response that uses all three "Rules for active listening".*

....

....

4 *Practice your active listening skills. Work in pairs. Take turns being the agent and the caller.*

Scenario 1

A very upset elderly lady has called to say that her husband died last month, and she has lost the insurance policy. She is very anxious because she does not know what the policy number is. You are able to find out the policy number by entering the husband's date of birth and address into your computer.

Scenario 2

An irate young professional has just called from New York complaining about his transatlantic flight booking. He is supposed to arrive in London at 1 p.m., not leave NYC at 1 p.m. The flight goes tomorrow and he has just discovered the mistake. He said this has happened before, and he is thinking of switching travel agents.

2 Checking information

An important part of active listening is checking information. Successful agents always check that the information they are noting is correct by paraphrasing and repeating back names, numbers, and other details:

Caller: *I'm calling because my daughter is ill. I need help with claim forms for her policy.*
Agent: *OK, so you're calling on behalf of your daughter. May I take her name?*
Caller: *Yes. Her name is Karen Mathews.*
Agent: *K-A-R-E-N M-A-T-H-E-W-S. Is that correct?*
Caller: *Yes, that's right.*

1 *Work in pairs. Without looking at each other, pretend to order a meal from a restaurant. The caller needs to include the following information. The agent needs to check all the information:*

- ◆ the order
- ◆ address
- ◆ a phone number
- ◆ brief directions to the office/house/classroom

D Pronunciation

1 Word stress and meaning (1)

Generally the words that are stressed in standard English are nouns, verbs, adjectives, and adverbs. This is because these words carry the most meaning.

- ◆ Words such as *the, a, an, and, in*, etc. are often less important and so will usually be unstressed.

- ◆ However, sometimes these "less important" words are stressed to make a particular point. For example, *Are you sure you put it **in** the box?* implies that the speaker thinks that the object may not have been put inside the box and wants to be sure.

 1 *Look at the agent's first sentence in your transcript and underline the words that you think will be stressed naturally. Remember, words that carry the most meaning are generally stressed. Listen to the sentence to check your answers, then practice saying it aloud.*

2 *Say the sentences below aloud to a partner, stressing the words in bold. Discuss the effect the different stresses have on the meaning. Then listen to more sentence pairs in Additional Listening.*

1. The bottle **is** empty.
2. The **bottle** is empty.
3. The bottle is **empty**.
4. **The** bottle is empty.

3 *Role-play a customer inquiry. The caller wants to return a faulty television, and the agent needs to check that the caller hasn't broken it him/herself. Do the role-play twice, once with the agent using word stress to sound pleasant, then using word stress to sound unpleasant. Discuss the differences.*

4 *Look at the words in bold and complete the interactions as in the example.*

1. Agent: *Did you say just your* husband has a phone, ma'am?...

   Caller: My husband and I **both** have phones.

2. Agent: ....

   Caller: Do **you** have a record of his Social Security number?

3. Agent: ....

   Caller: But I only got **two** thousand dollars!

4. Caller: ....

   Agent: We **did** send a reminder, sir.

5. Caller: ....

   Agent: I'm sorry, but I **can't** do that for you.

6. Caller: ....

   Agent: Would you like me to **block** your partner's access to this card?

5 *In pairs, say the sentences below aloud, stressing the words in bold. Write the meaning and a possible emotion or attitude for each sentence.*

Sentence	Meaning	Caller emotion/attitude
1. **I** don't have a policy number.	*Someone else might have the policy number.*	*Caller might feel defensive.*
2. I don't **have** a policy number.	_____	_____
3. I don't have a policy **number**.	_____	_____

THE ACCOUNT IS <u>NOW</u> FULLY PAID UP.

DOES THAT MEAN IT'S NOT GONNA BE PAID UP SOON? OR IT WASN'T PAID UP BEFORE?

THE MEANING OF WORD STRESS

E Read and explain

○ *Spend one minute skimming the text, and then complete the paired activities below.*

Mrs. A. Bookman
10 Louisiana Drive, Belvedere, Alabama

Dear Sir/Madam,

Cell Phone Plan Reference no. 4785960

I am writing to complain about the unsatisfactory service I have received from your company since I registered for a cell phone plan six months ago. I registered this scheme in both my husband's name, Mr. George Bookman, and my own, Adela Bookman.

We asked for your plan "Zero time - Zero cost" for both our phones, which included 300 minutes of voice time and 130 texts per month. We agreed to pay a flat amount of $45 per month, and the agreement stipulates that if we exceed that amount we pay a penalty amount of $25 per month.

Last month our teenage son (without our knowledge) used the text function on our phones and ran up 250 texts. Between us we also exceeded the maximum voice time by 50 minutes. Last month you sent us a bill of $90. I rang your customer service office and was told that there is an extra penalty amount if both voice and text exceed the agreed maximum amounts. I can find no reference to this in our contract. When I pointed this out to your call center agent, she insisted that the new company policy says that if we exceed both limits, there is this extra penalty amount. When I asked why we, the customers, were not informed about this, she said there was no legal requirement to do so. I find this difficult to believe.

As this amount has already been auto paid by my bank, I am writing to insist that the amount of $20 is immediately reimbursed to my account. If this is not done within a 10-day period, I will contact the Alternative Dispute Resolution (ADR) department.

I think it is unethical to change your policies without prior notification and agreement from your customers, and I expect this to be sorted out quickly.

Sincerely,

Adela Bookman

---

1 *Role-play these situations in pairs, as caller and agent. Swap roles for the second task.*

1. **Caller:** I am George Bookman and I know my wife sent a letter to you a few weeks ago. We've had an awful month because she was in a car accident and is in hospital with broken legs. Can you just summarize what our concern with your company is?

2. **Caller:** I am Adela Bookman's attorney. Can you fill me in on the details from the letter you received?

F Intercultural matters

1 Humor

■ Humor is an important part of American popular culture. American comedy shows have become globally successful, and comedy actors are some of the highest paid entertainers in the USA.

■ In call center exchanges, humor has a special function, which is essential to understand. It is used for two different purposes:
  ◆ to build rapport (using perhaps humorous comments or jokes),
  ◆ to express anger or annoyance using humorous comments or jokes insincerely. This function of humor is also known as *sarcasm* or *irony*.

1 *Work in pairs. Prepare mini call center scenarios (1–2 minutes) in which the caller uses humor to build rapport. Present your scenarios to other pairs. How important was the agent's response to the humor for successfully building rapport?*

2 Friendly or furious?

■ In the case of both rapport building and expressing anger, it is crucial that the humor used by the caller is correctly understood and appropriately responded to by the agent. Sometimes this can be confusing because when saying the same phrase, a slightly different tone can mean the difference between friendliness and fury (expressed through sarcasm). Here are some tips for correctly diagnosing humorous comments:

Think about the context: this will tell you a lot about whether humor is friendly or angry. For example, if a customer has been irate, but ends the call by saying *Thank you, you have been most helpful*, this is likely to be anger with the agent that he/she was not as helpful as the caller had hoped.

Listen to the tone: as you saw in Unit 4 section D, the tone of laughter and humorous comments will usually give away the caller's feelings. If the tone sounds annoyed, but the words are friendly, trust the tone!

1 *Match the caller statements with a context. What is the underlying meaning behind what the caller says in the three contexts? There is more than one possible combination of statement and context.*

Statement	Context
1. "I've been out shopping for my kids all day. My last card purchase was refused! I sometimes wish Santa Claus did exist. Christmas would be a lot cheaper!"	a) Caller has been on hold for a long time. b) Caller is asking to temporarily increase the credit limit on his/her card. c) The previous agent got the time difference wrong. The caller is complaining about this, while following up on the original inquiry.
2. "Don't hesitate to wake me up in the early hours of the morning when you get news on this."	d) Caller has been overcharged on his/her credit card. This was a mistake your company made. e) Caller is urgently waiting to hear about an insurance payout.
3. "Well this is fantastic. I hardly had to wait at all for service!"	f) Caller's issue was dealt with very quickly.

 2 *Listen to the start of the call from (line 1-40) and note down when you think the caller used humor to build rapport. Compare your notes with the class. Discuss how well the agent responded.*

3 *Listen to the call again and note the line numbers when the caller uses humor EITHER to build rapport OR to express displeasure. Then complete the table below.*

Caller uses humor to build rapport	Caller uses humor to express anger	Comments on agent's response	Improved response
Line 91: *We don't text message and nobody text messages us.*	—	*Agent ignored attempt to build rapport and went straight on with business saying: "Um ... oh, I understand ..."*	*Join in laughter, then say: "I'm not much of a texter either – it takes too long!"*

3 Responding to humor

- **Responding appropriately:** Once you have correctly diagnosed the meaning behind the humorous remark or laughter, you need to respond appropriately. Not doing so will either increase the caller's annoyance or cause you to miss an opportunity to build rapport. You cannot afford to do either!

- **Building relationships** with callers is an important part of achieving customer satisfaction, especially with American callers. It is crucial that as part of your customer service you are able to continue a joke or humorous small talk initiated by the caller.

- **Defusing anger communicated through humor:** The best way to do this is to not treat the humor as a joke, but to respond seriously to the real meaning behind it. For example, a caller who is annoyed that he was woken at 4 a.m. the last time he was called by the company, says: *"Don't hesitate to wake me up at 4 a.m. when you get news on this."* A model response would be: *"On behalf of the company, I'd like to sincerely apologize for that incident – I'll certainly make sure it **never** happens again!"*

1 *Work in pairs to create responses to the following humorous remarks from callers. Practice saying them aloud with the correct tone (sincerely apologetic or light and friendly).*

1. I feel like a tennis ball being hit back and forth, the way I'm being transferred from one department to the next! *(angry)*
2. You can call back any time; I'll be in all night. My social life is speaking to customer support representatives! *(building rapport)*
3. To "administer" an account that is used once a year and get 40 bucks for it! Wow, I should apply for that job! *(angry)*
4. My kids are away at college and my husband is always out, so it's like the farm animals are my family. I need medicine for Grandma Cow! *(building rapport)*

 **G** Role-play

○ *Work in groups of three. Read the scenario and your rolecard carefully, and act out the role-play.*

Scenario

A customer is calling because of charges for internet access on the cell phone. Telco, the cell phone company, provides calling plans and also sells plans which allow customers to browse the internet with their cell phones at reduced costs. If customers do not have the internet plan, accessing the internet can be very costly. The agent cannot grant a refund in this case. At the end of the role-play decide if the call was successful.

ROLECARD 1

Caller

You are an elderly person and you are calling Telco because you have a very high monthly bill on your cell phone resulting from internet charges. This is making you furious. You are refusing to pay this month's bill. Your regular plan is US$50 per month. US$20 have been added on top of your regular bill. You are unaware that cell phones access the internet and have never knowingly used this function. Remember that you are elderly and your hearing is very poor, and you do not understand technical jargon. Ask the agent to repeat things to you frequently.

ROLECARD 2

Agent

A confused and angry caller is complaining about high fees related to internet usage with the cell phone. The caller claims that he/she had no idea that the phone had the ability to access the internet. You must explain to the caller that:

* most modern phones are capable of internet access.
* even accidental internet access will incur charges.
* the caller is responsible for the charges incurred last month.

To avoid further internet charges you can offer:

* free internet for one month, or
* disable the internet function on the phone.

ROLECARD 3

Quality assurance personnel

Listen to the interaction between the agent and the caller. Fill out the form below, and then give the agent feedback after the call has finished.

Evaluate the agent		
Active listening	YES/NO	Notes:
Empathy	YES/NO	Notes:
Sincere apology	YES/NO	Why? / Why Not?
Caller satisfied?	YES/NO	Why? / Why Not?

H Self-evaluation

Tasks	Check	Comments (areas for self-improvement)
A The call Did you understand the purpose of the call and detailed information, with particular reference to the caller's emotions?	☐	_____
B Focus on language Are you confident about using modals to express obligation, the passive forms, and phrasal verbs?	☐	_____
C Soft skills Can you use active listening skills?	☐	_____
D Pronunciation Do you understand how word stress affects the meaning of a sentence?	☐	_____
E Read and explain Can you read, synthesize, and then tell someone what you have read?	☐	_____
F Intercultural matters Can you recognize humor and appropriately respond to it?	☐	_____
G Role-play For this unit overall, what were your strengths and weaknesses?		_____

7 Showing empathy

What you will learn!
At the end of this unit, you will have covered:

A The call: listening to understand the overall purpose and details of the call, as well as the feelings of the caller

B Focus on language: using the present continuous with *just*, *actually*, and *still* ◆ modals used in request ◆ phrasal verbs

C Soft skills: evaluating other agents ◆ building relationships ◆ showing empathy

D Pronunciation: differentiating vowel sounds

E Read and explain: reading and synthesizing information about getting a visa to explain to a customer in non-technical English

F Intercultural matters: litigation and compensation culture

G Role-play: simulating a call center transaction about problems with a flight reservation

I JUST HAD A TERRIBLE CALL! THE CUSTOMER WAS SO ANGRY.

OH, YOU POOR THING! DON'T WORRY. I'M SURE YOU'RE DOING A GREAT JOB.

I'M ON A BREAK. LET'S GO FOR A HOT CHOCOLATE.

I BET THE CALLERS LOVE YOU WITH THOSE EMPATHY SKILLS!

A The call

1 Pre-listening activity

The caller says "I just don't want to have to go to my lawyers on all these goof ups!"
What do you think the call will be about?

2 **Global listening activity**

 Listen to the call. As you listen, note down information about:

1. the personality and the emotional state of the caller.
2. what the main purpose of the call is.

Discuss your answers in groups.

3 **Detailed listening activity**

1 *Listen to the call again and discuss in pairs how the customer was feeling throughout this call. Did his emotions change? How? Why?*

2 *Plot how the emotions of the caller fluctuate during the call on the graph.*

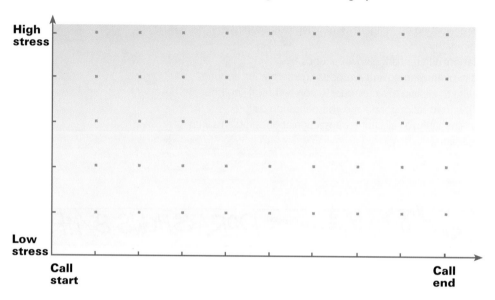

3 *Look at the transcript and write on the graph the line numbers where the caller's emotions change. Compare your graph with others.*

B Focus on language

1 **Present continuous (2)**

1 *The present continuous was practiced in Unit 2. Work in pairs. Do you remember the three functions of the present continuous?*

2 *Look at the examples of the present continuous from the call. Which function is each one an example of?*

1. **Caller:** I'm calling in reference to my policy.

    Function: ....

2. **Agent:** I'm going to put this to our Reinstatement Department.

    Function: ....

3. **Caller:** Someone's goofing up there and putting me through stress!

    Function: ....

3 *Look at the transcript and find further examples of the present continuous. Which functions do they demonstrate (1, 2, or 3)?*

2 Extended use of *just, actually,* and *still*

In Unit 2 we looked at the use of *just*. *Just* helps the agent (and sometimes the caller) to talk about the timing and intensity of something he/she has done or is about to do. It also helps to control the requests and feelings of the customer. *Actually* and *still* are two more words that improve control of emphasis. Compare these examples:

Well **actually** Ms. Wood, I am **still** trying to locate that reference number on the computer.

Well Ms. Wood, I am **still** trying to locate that reference number on the computer.

The first sentence emphasizes that the agent has understood the focus of the caller's concern. *Still* in the second part of the sentence shows that this effort has been happening for some time and continues.

1 *Find examples of* just, actually, *and* still *in the transcript and complete the table.*

Line number	Agent uses in order to …

2 *Work in pairs. Use* just, actually, *and* still *to respond to the following caller prompts.*

1. I thought you said that the check was already in the mail – where is it?
2. I made three bookings last week to fly to New York on the 25th. I've received only two e-tickets for the 26th.
3. Thanks for all your help. I'll expect to receive an application form in the mail next week.
4. How many days will it take to process this application?

3 Modals used in polite requests

Modal verbs can be used to make requests sound more polite. Compare these requests:

Repeat that, sir!
Would *you repeat that, sir?*
Could *you (possibly) repeat that, sir?*

1 *Write down as many different ways of making polite requests that you can think of. Share your answers with a partner, and discuss which you think sound the most polite and why. Remember that word stress and intonation can also make your requests sound polite, too.*

2 *Look at the transcript and highlight examples of polite requests.*

3 *Read the situations below and think of appropriate requests.*

1. You want to take an extra day off work to go away for a long weekend. Your supervisor has not been in a particularly good mood recently. What do you say?

   ....

2. You want to borrow your friend's camera for the weekend. She borrowed your camera recently and broke it, so she will be pleased to lend it to you. What do you say?

   ....

4 Phrasal verbs (4)

1 *In groups, brainstorm all the phrasal verbs you know that use the words* let *or* look. *Note their meaning in the table below.*

Let	Meaning	Look	Meaning
let off	*not punish*	*look out*	*find*

2 *Write three sentences using each phrasal verb. You may use more than one phrasal verb in each sentence.*

3 *Read the transcript of the call and write down any phrasal verbs that you find.*

Phrasal verb	Meaning

C Soft skills

1 Evaluating the agent

■ Communicating effectively in a call center environment requires very good "soft skills." You will need to be able to evaluate yourself and continually improve. The first step to doing this is to evaluate other agents.

1 *Read the transcript of the call center exchange and check true (T) or false (F) beside the "Agent evaluation".*
Give the transcript line numbers as evidence for your answers.

Agent evaluation	T	F	Line number(s)
1. Agent was able to solve the caller's problem.			
2. Agent communicated his solution to the customer's problem effectively.			
3. Agent was polite to the customer.			
4. Agent demonstrated he was listening carefully to the customer.			
5. Agent showed empathy for the concerns of the customer.			
6. Agent was always understood by the customer.			

2 Building relationships

■ An important soft skill is the ability to recognize *solidarity cues*. These will help you to effectively build good relationships with callers. Solidarity cues are things the caller says to be friendly and understanding. These may occur even if there are problems that cannot be solved:
This problem wasn't your fault, but I really need to get this booking done quickly. I know you understand that and you'll do your best for me, won't you?

1 *Look for examples of solidarity cues in the transcript and complete the table.*

Line number	Solidarity cues

3 Showing empathy

■ The concept of *empathy* has already been introduced in Units 4 and 6 as important for defusing anger and active listening. In this unit we will be looking at empathy in more detail.

■ Build a relationship with your caller by responding with empathy to problems or complaints:
Caller: I've been trying to get through to you for the last 30 minutes. I really don't have time to be put on hold because I have a job to do too, you know!
Agent: I'm so sorry about that – I completely understand why you'd be anxious to speak to someone. I'll do my best to help you with your concern as fast as possible, so you can get back to your work.

Some more empathetic responses :
That's a terrible thing to go through. I'm sorry to hear that.
I see what you mean. That would be very upsetting. Let me see what I can do …
Oh dear, that's awful! What can I do to help?

1 *Work in pairs. Read the caller problems and write empathetic responses. Practice saying them aloud and showing genuine empathy.*

1. I've just had my wallet stolen, and it has everything in it, including my credit card, so I'd like to cancel it.
2. My husband died last week, and I'm in a real mess about this insurance business. Do you think you can explain?
3. I'm on Highway 398 going south, and my car has overheated and there's smoke coming out of the hood. Can you send a tow truck out to give me a hand?

D Pronunciation

Differentiating vowel sounds (1)

■ Pronouncing vowel sounds correctly is an important part of being understood by callers. In this unit, the caller has difficulty understanding if the agent's name is *Dale* or *Dell*. This is because the agent uses the vowel sound /e/ (as in *Dell*, *sell*) instead of /eɪ/ (as in *Dale*, *sale*). The /eɪ/ sound is longer than the /e/ sound.

■ Another important vowel distinction is the long and short i-sound. There is a short /ɪ/ as in *tip*, and the longer /i:/ as in *feel*. The longer sound is made when your lips are spread as if you are smiling. Study the examples in the table below.

short /ɪ/ sound	long /i:/ sound
fill	feel
big	steal
still	real
rip	deal

1 *Work in pairs. Find words in the transcript with the same sound and add them to the table below. Say the words aloud to one another to check your answers.*

/eɪ/	/e/	/ɪ/	/i:/
Dale	Dell	fill	feel

2 *Work in pairs. Sit back-to-back, each with the table below. Student A reads aloud one word from each pair. Student B highlights the words. Check the words you highlighted. Swap roles and repeat.*

deep	dip
fail	fell
steal	still
date	debt
peel	pill
late	let
eat	it
mate	met
keen	kin
later	letter

3 *Tongue twisters. Say this sentence aloud:*

Ian checked into an inn to meet a mate.

Write five more tongue twisters using the four vowel sounds in this section. Use different words.

E Read and explain

○ *Spend one minute skimming the text, and then complete the paired activities below.*

Getting a Visa

General information
The cost for a visa is around US$50 and the processing time is a matter of days. Express visas can be completed in one day, but there is an additional cost for this service.

Normally visas will be single entry and valid for 30 days, although multiple-entry visas are also available for a longer period and will cost more. While it may be possible to secure a visa on arrival, it is recommended that travelers get their visas in advance to avoid disappointment.

There are many categories of visa types as outlined below.

Visa categories
F-type visa: the visa for doing business
This type of visa is suitable for visitors who intend to:
1. do business (e.g., sign agreements, procure products and services, set up a company);
2. take an internship for less than 6 months;
3. give an educational lecture, or engage in other kinds of academic exchange.
Normally a one-way visa will be issued for a period of a 30-day stay, and must be used within 90 days of the visa's being issued.

L-type visa: the visa for tourists/visitors
This type of visa is suitable for visitors who want to sightsee and/or visit relatives and friends. Normally this will be a one-way visa and will be issued for a period of a 30-day stay, and must be used within 90 days of issue. You may apply for a longer "Duration of Stay" from a local visa office when you arrive if you want to extend your stay for another 30-day period.

Z-type visa: the visa for working abroad
This type of visa will be issued to an alien who has already secured employment. This type of visa will also be issued to his/her immediate family. It is normally issued for one entry for three months. The holder of this visa will be subject to completing residential formalities at the local public security department within 30 days of arrival.

There are other, less common, visa types that the Immigration Department at your closest embassy can provide information about.

Visa Application Forms can be downloaded through your embassy website.

1 *Role-play these situations in pairs. The agent uses the visa information on the last page to explain clearly what kind of visa the caller needs. Give all the relevant information without reading directly from the text. Swap roles for the second caller.*

1. **Caller:** Good morning! I've just got a job abroad for 12 months and I'd like to know what kind of visa I'll need to take my family with me.

2. **Caller:** I'm hoping to backpack and sightsee for about three months. Can you tell me what kind of visa I'll need, and what it is likely to cost?

2 *Work in groups of three. Each person takes one visa category type to read for one minute. After one minute, close your book, and tell your group the requirements for the visa category you have just read about.*

F Intercultural matters

1 Litigation and compensation culture

■ The United States has more lawyers per capita than any other country. In this unit we will be looking at civil lawsuits. Civil cases involve disputes between individuals and/or companies in which the victim may be awarded compensation. For example, if a car crash victim claims financial compensation from the driver for injury as a result of the accident, this would be a civil case.

■ Americans spend more on civil cases than any other nation. Lawyers for these cases earned an estimated US$40 billion in awards in 2002. One high-profile civil case against a company was when McDonald's fast food chain was ordered by a court to pay an 81-year-old woman US$2.9 million because she was burned when she spilled her McDonald's coffee.

■ A high percentage (94%) of Americans in a recent survey think that there is an increasing tendency for people to threaten legal action when something goes wrong. Most of those surveyed think that the justice system is used by many people as a lottery – they start a lawsuit just to see how much they can win.

1 *Read about the lawsuits and give your opinion of the judgments and the compensation awarded.*

Lawsuit	Your opinion
1. A woman in Pennsylvania was awarded US$113,500 in damages after she slipped on a spilled soft drink and broke her tailbone. The woman had thrown the drink at her boyfriend 30 seconds earlier during an argument.	
2. A man in California was awarded US$55,000 by the local government when he fell into a hole in the pavement and broke both legs and wrists in several places. The hole had been covered with tarpaulin by builders so that it looked like there was no hole.	
3. A woman in St. Louis was awarded US$6,000 when she sued a hair salon because she claimed that a bad hair treatment in which her hair turned green and partially fell out had caused her emotional distress, depression, and loss of income.	
4. A woman in Austin successfully sued a furniture store after she broke her ankle tripping over a toddler. The toddler was in fact the woman's son.	
5. A Virginia woman successfully sued her company for unfair dismissal when she was fired by text message because she did not come to a company social event. She was reinstated in her position and awarded US$18,000.	
6. A Delaware man successfully sued a nightclub for US$12,000 after he fell through a bathroom window and broke his two front teeth. The accident occurred while the man was trying to sneak through the bathroom window to avoid the US$3.50 cover charge.	

2 *In groups, think of three more examples where a civil case might be filed. How much compensation do you think the victim should receive? Discuss with other groups.*

2 Dealing with customer dissatisfaction

■ The litigation and compensation culture of the Western world, particularly in the United States, is rooted in the following formula:

Dissatisfaction = Somebody is responsible = I deserve compensation

■ Dissatisfaction can arise from many different things, but the typical reason for a caller to feel dissatisfied to the point of threatening legal action is if the quality of service does not meet his/her expectations. This is why it is so important to keep in mind American expectations of customer service when you are speaking to an American caller.

1 *Listen to the call and read the transcript again. Note in the table below when the caller expresses displeasure at the service and the agent's response. Suggest improved responses.*

Caller displeasure		Agent response		Improved response
Somebody's got a case of incompetence. *(line 123)*	➡		➡	
	➡		➡	
	➡		➡	
	➡		➡	

2 *Look at the "Business / Service expectations" below and rank them on a scale of 1 to 5 (5 is the highest). Compare with your partner or group and explain your choices.*

Business / Service expectations	Importance to Americans	Importance to your culture
Making small talk	_____	_____
Accuracy and not making mistakes	_____	_____
Punctuality	_____	_____
Direct answers to direct questions	_____	_____
Taking responsibility for mistakes	_____	_____

3 *Work in pairs. Role-play the situations below. The agent must use his/her cultural awareness of American callers to handle the complaint. Swap roles and repeat.*

1. The caller is angry because the last agent he/she spoke to promised to call back at 10 a.m. It is now 10:15 and he/she has not received a call.

2. The caller is complaining that his/her order was made two months ago and every time the caller has followed-up on the order, he/she has been told that a status report would be emailed. No email has arrived. Caller feels that he/she is not being told the truth. The truth is that the agent handling this caller's order did not log the information accurately. This agent has recently been dismissed from the company and you are responsible for taking over his work.

G Role-play

○ *Work in groups of four. Read the scenario carefully. Two members of the group sit back-to-back and play the roles of caller and agent. The other two members peer-evaluate using the score sheet. The candidates also self-evaluate using the score sheet. Swap roles and repeat.*

Scenario

The Smith family are planning to travel from New York City to Shanghai next week. Mr. and Mrs. Smith have received the e-tickets on their home computer. They have been using Pan China Air Travel Agency to make all the flight and hotel bookings, but it has been problematic. Now Mr. and Mrs. Smith have discovered that one of their children has no flight ticket at all, and the other child has been booked as an adult. They are also a vegetarian family and need special food on the flight. The family needs visas, but the travel agency has not provided any information or assistance with this.

ROLECARD I	ROLECARD 2
Caller	**Agent**
You are feeling fed up as the travel agency has provided very little efficient service so far, and the vacation is supposed to start next week. There are three main things to sort out during this call: 1. The children's bookings need to be corrected. 2. Check vegetarian meals ordered. 3. Find out what needs to be done to secure the tourist visa for China. Make a list of other things that you are worried about.	You have a customer who is feeling fed up because there are problems with the bookings and Express Chinese visas are required. The colleague who took the original call has now left Pan China Agency. He/She was a bit lazy, and you now have to work very hard to assist this family. Write down ideas/expressions you may want to use with this caller.

Evaluate the agent		
Did the agent use active listening?	YES/NO	Notes:
Did the agent show empathy?	YES/NO	Notes:
Did the agent handle all of the problems?	YES/NO	Why? / Why Not?
Will the customer need to call back about these issues?	YES/NO	Why? / Why Not?
Did the agent use solidarity cues to show willingness to help?	YES/NO	List the cues here:

 **H** Self-evaluation

Tasks	Check	Comments (areas for self-improvement)
A The call Did you understand the purpose of the call and detailed information, with particular reference to the caller's emotions?	☐	
B Focus on language Are you confident about using the present continuous? How about using modals to make polite requests? And phrasal verbs?	☐	
C Soft skills Are you confident about building relationships and showing empathy?	☐	
D Pronunciation Can you differentiate between vowel sounds?	☐	
E Read and explain Can you read, synthesize, and then tell someone what you have read?	☐	
F Intercultural matters Do you understand the culture of litigation and compensation in the USA? Can you respond to complaints in a culturally intelligent manner?	☐	
G Role-play For this unit overall, what were your strengths and weaknesses?		

8 Thinking aloud and building solidarity

What you will learn!
At the end of this unit, you will have covered:

A The call: listening to understand the overall purpose and details of the call, as well as the feelings of the caller

B Focus on language: modals used to express ability ◆ using the first conditional for instructions

C Soft skills: letting the customer know what you are thinking ◆ building solidarity through *we* and *us* pronouns

D Pronunciation: intonation when giving instructions ◆ intonation and context

E Read and explain: reading and synthesizing information about IT services to explain to a customer in non-technical English

F Intercultural matters: self-empowerment and self-reliance culture

G Role-play: simulating a call center transaction about using certain features of a computer

DAN and DORA - KEEP THE CALLER INFORMED!

I'M IN RETRAINING BECAUSE MY QA SCORES WERE DOWN.

I HAVE TO LEARN ABOUT "THINKALOUD"!

YEAH, THE CUSTOMER LIKES TO KNOW WHAT'S GOING ON!

I DON'T THINK MY CUSTOMERS WOULD LIKE TO HEAR EVERYTHING I THINK ...

A The call

1 Pre-listening activity

The caller says "I don't like paying for service I can't even get."
What do you think the call will be about?

2 Global listening activity

Listen to the call and say whether the statements below are true (T) or false (F):

1. The caller remains angry throughout the call. .... ☐
2. The agent is patient with the caller. .... ☐
3. The problem is resolved at the end of the call. .... ☐
4. The caller has a basic knowledge of using computers. .... ☐
5. The agent and caller share a joke during the call. .... ☐

3 Detailed listening activity

Listen to the call again and complete the table below in your own words:

What is the problem?	What is the solution?

B Focus on language

1 Modals of ability

> ▣ We use *can* and *be able to* to talk about our ability to do things:
> I **can get** this finished before I leave the office.
> I **won't be able to get** that done before I go home.
>
> ▣ In the past:
> I **could swim** when I was only three years old.
> I **was able to get** it done before I went home.
> If you hadn't interrupted me, I **could have finished** before I left the office last night. (It didn't happen.)

1 Complete the following sentences with modals of ability.

1. I .... buy your tickets this morning because I didn't take enough money with me.
2. If you had sent in the right address, I .... sent your credit card out last week.
3. We .... certainly process your claim right away as long as I have your Social Security number.
4. .... you give this back and make an immediate refund?
5. I .... suggested a different package if I'd known her family was so big.

2 Read the transcript and highlight examples of modals of logical deduction (covered in Unit 4) and modals of ability.

2 Using the first conditional for instructions

> ▣ The first conditional can be used as a polite way of giving instructions.
> **If** you **click** on the icon, you **'ll get** in immediately.
>
> ▣ It is formed with:
>
> | if + simple present (clause 1) | will + verb (clause 2) |
> |---|---|

1 *Give instructions to your partner using the first conditional for the situations below.*

1. Exercising to lose weight
2. Studying hard to get onto a college course
3. Saving money to buy a house
4. Starting work on time to complete all your tasks

 2 *Listen to the call again and note down examples of the first conditional for giving instructions.*

C Soft skills

1 Thinking aloud professionally

■ When you are helping a caller with a problem, it is reassuring and helpful for him/her to be talked through the process of problem solving. Remember that the caller can't see what you are doing, or know what you are thinking – a silence is not reassuring! You can involve the customer by thinking aloud. We call this soft skill *professional thinkaloud*.

■ Examples of professional thinkaloud:
Let me just check that for you because I think it could be that …
I'm not sure; I'll have to check, but it sounds to me like …
We don't know for sure at this stage, but it may be that …
On the one hand it could be that you have gone over your credit limit; on the other it may be that there is an error in our system. Either way …

1 *Work in pairs. Role-play the following scenarios using professional thinkaloud.*

Scenario 1
Caller has a problem connecting his printer to his computer. You think it could be related to one of several problems: power lines, software, or a faulty printer.

Scenario 2
Caller says her sister is using her credit card without her permission. You are not sure of the procedure here, but you will need to gather some information and then pass over to a supervisor.

Scenario 3
Caller is calling from China. Her camera has been stolen along with some other expensive electronic items. These were all insured through your company. She wants to know whether she has to register the theft with the local police.

2 Building solidarity through the pronouns *we* and *us*

■ The use of the pronouns *we* and *us* rather than *you* helps to build solidarity between the agent and the caller, giving the impression that the problem is shared. By sharing the problem, you not only build solidarity with your callers, but also reassure them that their problems will be taken seriously.

1 *Look at the agent responses below. Which one builds solidarity better?*

Caller: I've lost my credit card. In fact, I think it's just been stolen. Help!
Agent: a) What you need to do is call the hotline immediately. .... ☐

   b) What we need to do is get connected to our hotline immediately. .... ☐

2 *Give responses using **we** and **us** to build solidarity and reassure customers.*

1. I forgot to pay my credit card this month. What can I do?
2. My computer has just crashed, and it has all my data on it!
3. I paid for flowers to be sent to my girlfriend on Valentine's Day, but I've just talked to her on the phone – she hasn't got them! This is a disaster!
4. My cell phone won't turn on, and I only bought it yesterday from one of your stores.

D Pronunciation

1 Intonation when giving instructions

■ Correct intonation is very important in communication. Inappropriate intonation can result in confusion and communication breakdown, or even offend the customer.

■ Generally, high voice tone and rising intonation sound more polite and sincere. A flat voice tone with no rising intonation can sound direct and critical.

1 *Look at the following exchange and role-play it with a partner in two different ways. First the agent should use intonation to sound helpful and sincere. The second time the agent should sound direct and critical (something that an agent should never do!).*

Agent: What seems to be the problem, sir?
Caller: Well, my monitor is blurry.
Agent: Have you tried turning it off and on again?
Caller: Yes, I have and it is still blurry.
Agent: I see. Then go to the panel at the bottom of the monitor and open it.
Caller: OK, and then …?

 2 *Listen to the call center exchange in Additional Listening 1. Discuss how intonation affects meaning.*

3 *Work in pairs. Read the transcript of the call, and highlight examples of the agent giving instructions. Say the phrases aloud to each other with sincere and helpful intonation.*

 4 *Listen to the call again and rate the agent's intonation when she gives the caller instructions on a scale of 1 to 3 for appropriateness (3 is the highest). Explain your scores to a partner.*

5 *Work in pairs. Your trainer will give you role cards. Sit back-to-back and do not look at each other's role card. Use the appropriate intonation for the context. Remember your listening skills!*

6 *Give your partner feedback on his/her intonation. Did you feel he/she was sincere and interested?*

2 Intonation and context

1 *Listen to the three versions of this dialog (Additional Listening 2) Who is speaking each time?*

A: I have something I need to tell you.
B: What is it?
A: I'm moving to another country.
B: Really?

a) Two good friends that have known each other for ten years .... ☐

b) A couple who will have to break up because a new job is more important than the relationship .... ☐

c) Two acquaintances; one of them is very happy to be moving .... ☐

2 *In each of the three dialogs, how do the speakers use intonation to express their different emotions? Discuss with a partner.*

3 *Work in pairs. Think of three different contexts for each of the following dialogs. Say them aloud and note how the intonation changes.*

1. A: I'm here now.
   B: Really, already?
   A: Yes … is that OK?
   B: Yes, sure. Just come see me in a few minutes.

2. A: What did you do that for?
   B: Oh, I thought it was a good idea.
   A: Really?
   B: Yes. What do you think about it?

3. A: How come it never works?
   B: I don't know.
   A: Hmm, I really wish it would work.
   B: Have you tried turning it on?

 **E** Read and explain

○ *Spend one minute skimming the text, and then complete the paired activities below.*

> **Getting the most out of your IT investment for your business with IT Auditing Inc.**
> **Do you understand the value of your IT systems to your business bottom line?**
> **Do you understand how you can harness IT to reach your business objectives?**
>
> IT professionals in your organization, while understanding the latest technology and software programs, often don't understand the management's business goals.
>
> IT Auditing Inc. seeks to bring technology planning and business planning together to ensure alignment and shared goals. We use a framework that ensures IT business investment decisions are well integrated into the daily operations of the business.
>
> IT Auditing Inc. suggests the following process to achieve alignment:
>
> **STEP 1**
> Get your key business management group committed to the value of an IT audit. Remember, IT professionals do not determine business strategies, nor do the operational managers know the range of IT choices available.
>
> **STEP 2**
> Ask these *four* key questions:
> Are we doing the right things? *(business strategy)*
> Are we getting the benefit? *(business value)*
> Are we doing it the right way? *(business architecture)*
> Are we getting it all done well? *(business deliverables)*
>
> **STEP 3**
> IT Auditing Inc. will then analyze the key processes in the business. For example, we will observe how business transactions are initiated, forms filled in, and inquiry calls taken. We will also observe:
> - Data entry processes and authorization for the next steps.
> - Service delivery: dispatch of goods.
> - Quality assurance mechanisms to ensure customer satisfaction.
> - Annual reporting of business volume and service level satisfaction.
>
> **STEP 4**
> IT Auditing Inc. will consult managers to gather input for improved processes.
>
> **STEP 5**
> Report and presentation including recommendations for IT improvements and streamlining.
>
> Cost is determined by business size and operational complexity. Make an appointment for a free one-hour consultation. Email us at: *itauditme@com* or call 800 658 2696.

1 *Role-play these situations in pairs. The agent should use the information on the last page to explain clearly how IT Auditing Inc. can help the caller. Give all the relevant information without reading directly from the text. Swap roles for the second caller.*

1. **Caller:** My business is expanding and I keep having to take on more administrative staff to process all the paperwork. Can you help me get more efficiency into my business?

2. **Caller:** My business is in a mess and I need to develop better strategies to achieve much better customer satisfaction. Can you help?

F Intercultural matters

1 Diagnosing self-reliant customers

■ If you are working for a company that provides technical support for electronic equipment (such as computers, phones, cameras, or music players), it is important to be skilled in quickly finding out how competent and self-reliant your customer is.

■ Some customers may want you to take on the problem completely, while others will want the opportunity to discuss each move, and to be proactive in sharing the problem-solving experience. Misdiagnosing this can cause anxiety and friction.

■ It is vital that you adapt your communication to take this into account. For less technically experienced customers you will need to use plain English (not technical jargon), whereas you may annoy technically experienced customers by over-explaining very familiar concepts.

1 *Look at the excerpt from another call below and answer the discussion questions in small groups.*

Caller: I can't get my documents to print; the screen just freezes.
Agent: OK, sir, I'd like to check a few things before we get started. First, did you plug your computer in?
Caller: Of course I plugged it in …
Agent: OK, then, second –
Caller: Look, I don't mean to be rude, but can we cut to the chase. I just need to know if this problem can be solved over the phone, or I'll need to take it in.
Agent: Yes, sir, so, then I need to just know if you have turned your printer on, sir?
Caller: Yes. *(laughs)* I've also tried rebooting and have repaired all the network connections.

1. How well did the agent diagnose the competency and self-reliance of the caller?
2. What did the caller say to give clues about his competence and self-reliance?
3. How do you think the caller felt?
4. How would you improve the agent's performance?

2 *Look at the transcript of this unit's call and highlight where the caller gives clues about how self-reliant he wants to be. Compare your answers with a partner.*

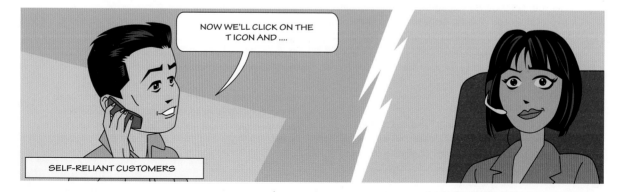

2 Self-empowerment culture

- American culture is founded on a strong belief in self-reliance and self-empowerment. It is a cultural expectation that people should be able to realize their ambitions on their own. The American Dream is based on the idea that anyone can become successful, regardless of where he/she comes from.

- Government support structures in the United States demonstrate this culture of self-reliance. Education and health-care support from the government is lower than in most other countries in the Western world. Below is a comparison of the USA and the UK.

Health care
UK: Fully government funded (free for everyone).
USA: Government helps with some services for the poor and elderly (everyone else pays).

Education
UK: College is heavily subsidized (highest tuition fees are around US$6,000 per year).
USA: College is partially subsidized (highest tuition fees are around US$30,000 per year).

Taxes in the United States are lower than in most other countries in the Western world, giving Americans more freedom to support themselves, and to use their own money for what is important to them.

1 *In groups of three, read the roles below. Then sit back-to-back and role-play the situation.*

Agent:
You have been asked to teach the caller how to use a USB (universal serial bus) cable to transfer photographs from a camera to a computer.

Caller:
You have a new camera and you have never used your computer to look at photos. You are very familiar with how to use your computer for other processes, and you have used other transferring devides (such as CDs) before. Because these pieces of equipment belong to you, you want to feel in control of using them and problem solving. You believe you can do anything you put your mind to!

Quality assurance:
- Note down language used by the agent to make the caller feel empowered.
- Note down any language used by the caller that communicates how competent he/she is.
- Evaluate how well the agent diagnosed the caller's competence and used that information in the explanation.

2 *Read the transcript. Note down the line numbers where the caller expresses feelings about empowerment (either low or high). Compare your notes with your partner and justify your choices.*

3 *Work in pairs. Evaluate the agent's responses in the call to the caller's expressions of low empowerment and suggest improvements (if applicable).*

Caller feeling disempowered (line number)		Evaluation of agent response		Improved agent response
	➧		➧	
	➧		➧	
	➧		➧	
	➧		➧	

G Role-play

○ *Work in pairs. Read the scenario and your rolecard carefully, and act out the role-play.*

Scenario

A sales executive needs a walkthrough which will enable him/her to download a document and then print it. Giving technical instructions is a difficult process, but something that support staff pride themselves on doing well. Some callers are more familiar with technical terms than others. The agent must make sure that the caller is one hundred percent clear and will not be calling again.

ROLECARD 1

Caller

You work in sales for a big firm. You recently purchased a new computer made by a different company from the one you were used to. It uses different software and has a totally different layout from your old computer. You do not understand how to use it, and it is making you very confused and worried.

You have been sent a presentation via email and you need to prepare for it. You have to:

♦ download the file from your webmail, and
♦ print that document so you can prepare properly.

You are calling technical support to ask them for assistance. You do not have a product registration number. You only have the computer in front of you. This is a new type of computer with unfamiliar software, so you don't understand any jargon specific to this computer or software. Whenever the agent uses a term you do not understand, you must ask him/her to clarify it for you.

ROLECARD 2

Agent

You work in technical support for a hardware and software manufacturer. A caller needs assistance with a rather simple procedure. You need to instruct the caller on how to download a file from a webmail server, and then print that document. Before giving the instructions you must verify that this caller has genuinely purchased a computer and original software from your company. You must ask for a product registration number. Once you have these details, give detailed and accurate instructions. Here are the steps you will need to explain to the caller:

1. Check that all cabling is properly connected.
2. Turn on computer and printer.
3. Access the internet by opening the browser menu and choosing ZapWeb.
4. Sign into ZapMail (the webmail on the computer).
5. Open email with attached document.
6. Download document.
7. Open document.
8. Print document.

Evaluate the agent		
Active listening	YES/NO	Notes:
Use of non-technical English (no jargon)	YES/NO	Notes:
Clear explanation	YES/NO	Notes:
Did customer understand the first time?	YES/NO	Why? / Why Not?

H Self-evaluation

Tasks	Check	Comments (areas for self-improvement)
A The call Did you understand the purpose of the call and detailed information, with particular reference to the caller's emotions?	☐	
B Focus on language Are you able to use modals of ability? Can you use the first conditional to give instructions?	☐	
C Soft skills Are you confident about using *professional thinkaloud*? Can you effectively build solidarity by using the pronouns *we* and *us*?	☐	
D Pronunciation Can you recognize different contexts from the intonation of the speakers?	☐	
E Read and explain Can you read, synthesize, and then tell someone what you have read?	☐	
F Intercultural matters Are you able to use your knowledge of American self-empowerment culture to positively impact calls?	☐	
G Role-play For this unit overall, what were your strengths and weaknesses?		

9 Keeping control of an aggressive call

What you will learn!
At the end of this unit, you will have covered:

A The call: listening to understand the overall purpose and details of the call, as well as the feelings of the caller

B Focus on language: expressing regret using the third conditional or *should have done* ◆ comparisons ◆ using idioms and phrasal verbs

C Soft skills: responding to an angry caller by defusing, apologizing, and keeping control of the call

D Pronunciation: interpreting caller attitude and emotion through word stress

E Read and explain: reading and synthesizing information about insurance claims to explain to a customer in non-technical English

F Intercultural matters: direct answers to direct questions ◆ saying *no*

G Role-play: simulating a call center transaction about billing address changes

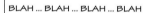

DAN and DORA – TAKE CONTROL OF THE CALL

A The call

1 Pre-listening activity

The caller says "I'd love to put someone in jail for this!"
What do you think the call will be about?

2 Global listening activity

 Listen to the call and choose the best adjectives to describe the caller and agent.

robotic	angry	polite	professional	persistent
unpleasant	upset	satisfied	helpful	timid
intimidated	threatening	concerned	incompetent	rude
frustrated	unhelpful	disinterested	expert	aggressive

Caller	Agent

3 Detailed listening activity

 Listen to the call again and choose the best answers to the questions below.

1. The caller says the insurance company has called
   a) twice this week.
   b) once this week.
   c) only that day.
   d) None of the above.

2. The caller doesn't know
   a) her father's date of birth.
   b) her father's Social Security number.
   c) both of the above.
   d) how to spell her father's name.

3. According to the agent, the check for US$9.92 was
   a) to cover the payout of a claim.
   b) to cover a discrepancy amount in the claim.
   c) instead of the US$800 check.
   d) requested by the caller's father.

4. Based on the call, the caller was upset about the US$800 check because
   a) she doesn't have much money at the moment.
   b) it was sent to the wrong address.
   c) she never received it.
   d) she thought the agent was being dishonest.

5. The agent says the reason for the call was
   a) to verify the address.
   b) to check the caller received the full amount of money.
   c) to get the birth date and Social Security number of the caller's father.
   d) to inform the caller that the case has gone to the Research Department.

6. The caller wants to speak to the supervisor because
   a) she thinks the agent is being dishonest about her check for US$800.
   b) she is frustrated by the incompetence of the agent.
   c) she thinks she may have lost the check.
   d) None of the above.

B Focus on language

1 Expressing regret

▪ The third conditional or *should have done* can be used to express regret:
*If I **had studied** harder, I **would have gotten** into college.*
*I have no money. I **shouldn't have bought** so many clothes last month.*

1 *Use the third conditional and* should have done *to express regret about the following situations.*

1. You forgot to turn off the oven and the kitchen caught fire.
    If I hadn't forgotten to turn off the oven, the kitchen wouldn't have caught fire.
    I should have turned off the oven. Then the kitchen wouldn't have caught fire.
2. You were driving too fast and crashed into another car.
3. You left your MP3 player in the restaurant when you went to the bathroom, and it was stolen.
4. You forgot to set your alarm clock and were late for work.
5. You didn't cook the meat properly and were ill that night.

2 *Work in pairs. Look at the transcript and find examples where either the caller or the agent expresses regret. Which was used more often: the third conditional or* should have done?

2 Making comparisons

▪ Making comparisons is very useful when talking to customers on the phone. Look at these examples:
*There are lots of software programs around, but Exped is **the best** if you want real value for the money.*
*I want to talk to someone **higher** up!*
*The quality of the photographs is not **as good as** we would like, but they're **the most detailed ones** we can generate on that computer.*
*The service was much **better than** I expected, but there is still room for improvement.*

1 *Work in pairs. Look at the statements below and make comparisons.*

1. Your hotel room is not very comfortable. Last time you stayed in this hotel, the room was very comfortable.
    This room is not as comfortable as the last room we had. / The last room we had was more comfortable than this room.

2. You would like improved service in your hotel.

3. You think the food is very bad at this restaurant.

4. You have never had such an uncomfortable plane trip in your life.

5. You just attended a very good concert. The last one you went to was terrible.

6. The test was very easy. You expect to get a high score.

3 Idioms and phrasal verbs

1 *Write the meanings of the idioms and phrasal verbs used in the call.*

Idioms/Phrasal verbs	Meaning
Let's **go through** this one more time.	_____
I'll **narrow down the search**.	_____
It's not **coming up in our system**.	_____
How did you **come up** with US$9.92?	_____
This **answer you're giving me is not flying**.	_____
I'll **be out** by US$800.	_____

2 *Here are more examples of idiomatic language used in call center interactions. Give the meanings.*

Idiom	Meaning
We'll just **bypass** that procedure.	_____
The program **kicks in** after you log in.	_____
Do you wanna **double-check** that?	_____
I just don't have the strength to **go through** all this again.	_____
We'll **get back on track** in a minute.	_____
The policy is **good through** January.	_____

3 *Work in pairs. Role-play a short call center exchange, using at least three of the idioms/phrasal verbs above.*

C Soft skills

1 Keeping control of an aggressive call

■ In Unit 4 you were introduced to some strategies for dealing with irritated callers. Dealing with angry callers, in this case an extremely angry caller, worries agents because conflict is hard to handle on the phone. This unit gives you more practice in this area.

■ Many new agents worry about angry callers. When a new agent has an angry caller, he/she may respond with silence – a very bad move! It is important to learn not to take personally what angry or frustrated callers say. Apologize and keep control of the call. To do this effectively you need the soft skills you have already learned about.

■ When apologizing in order to sound sincere, it is important to get the strength and wording of your apology right for the situation. For example, if you say you are *deeply sorry* for mishearing a number read aloud to you, the apology is too strong for the situation. If you say: *Oh, sorry about that* when someone has lost crucial documents because their computer crashed, the apology is too weak for the situation, and you will sound careless.

■ **Keeping control of a call: the dos and don'ts**
  1. Listen carefully to the caller's complaint and understand the cause of the anger. This may involve letting your callers "vent" his/her feelings. You can use this time to gather important information about the caller (emotion, purpose of call, expectations).

2. Acknowledge the caller's anger by saying:
I can see why that would be frustrating.
This will reassure the caller that you have listened and engaged with the reason he/she is annoyed.

3. Empathize with the caller. This will help to build solidarity with your caller because you are sharing his/her emotion.
I would be upset too if that had happened to me.

4. Apologize in an appropriate way. If you or your company has made a mistake, it is very important to apologize for it.
I'm sorry that happened to you.

5. Once you understand the problem and have reacted appropriately, you should take control of the situation by defining your role as a problem solver. Then focus on the purpose of the call.
I'm sorry that happened to you, **but I'm here to help put it right**, so let's …

6. Offer realistic solutions. Make promises that you can deliver.
What I can do is hand this on to someone else who …

7. Don't be silent. Your caller will want his/her anger to be acknowledged verbally.

8. Don't ask the caller to calm down or stop shouting. In this call, for example, the caller responds:
You know what? At this point, that's probably the most ridiculous thing you could tell me.

1 *Work in pairs. Look at the phrases below. Complete the sentences and find a context for each in which they would be appropriate. Practice using word stress and intonation to sound more sincere.*

1. I'm sorry ....

2. I apologize ....

3. I am deeply sorry ....

4. Sorry about that ....

5. I do apologize ....

6. Please excuse me ....

7. I'm so sorry ....

2 *Look at the transcript and note down times when the agent should have apologized, but didn't.*

3 *Work in pairs. Decide how strong the apology should be for the caller comments below on a scale of 1 to 5, with 5 being the strongest. Write your own apologies, then compare with a partner.*

1. Look, I'm so sick of calling you people over and over again to get support for the same damn problem. This is the second time you've charged me for support, and you haven't given me anything!

2. I called earlier and was told I'd get a call back within 10 minutes. It's now been 15 minutes and I haven't heard back, so I'm calling again.

3. The username and password your company issued for webpage access doesn't work! I've been trying to log on all morning, and it keeps saying they are invalid.

4. Could it be any slower?! First I waited for 15 minutes, only to be transferred to another department, and waited 15 minutes more. You've kept me on hold for another 10, doing I don't know what … and I'm paying you for this! I have a meeting in 25 minutes, and I want this issue resolved by then.

5. I've been trying to sort out my accounts since my husband died a year ago, but they seem to be in a terrible mess, and I haven't gotten anyone to give me a straight answer yet.

2 Sounding "robotic"

■ One of the complaints that callers often make of agents is that they sound "robotic." One caller described her experience as similar to "talking into a machine." Remember that callers like to feel that they are being listened to properly.

1 *Look through the transcript and underline the places where you think the agent sounded "robotic." In pairs, discuss how you might improve those responses.*

D Pronunciation

1 Word stress and meaning (2)

■ In this unit we will look again at the importance of word stress (see also Unit 6). We will be looking at word stress and meaning to help you communicate with customers.

■ Words that are stressed carry particular meaning. For example:
Agent: *Well Ms. Granthan, I've got on record that we got an email from you about an hour ago, but –*
Caller: *I just **called** about 60 minutes ago.*
The caller wants to emphasize that she called recently. The word stress shows that she is correcting the agent and wants to insist that a call was made, not an email.

■ Mastering interpretation of word stress will give you great insight into how a caller is feeling, which in turn can give you clues about how to respond appropriately to defuse anger, reassure, or empathize.

1 *In pairs, read what the callers below say and think what the agent may have said to "trigger" the word stress. Then write an appropriate response.*

1. I have **never** missed a payment.
2. So what do **you** plan to do about this?
3. That's not **my** fault!
4. How **long** do I have to wait?

2 *The meaning of the caller quote below is different if different words are stressed. In groups, highlight the words that can be stressed and identify the different meanings. Then practice saying the sentences aloud.*

Caller: You really should've done that.

1. ....
2. ....
3. ....
4. ....
5. ....

3 *In pairs, read aloud the sentences below, stressing the words in bold. Student B listens and writes down what he/she thinks the stress means (attitude, emotion, and context). Swap roles and repeat.*

Student A to read aloud:
1. What **can** he do?
2. She **said** she is leaving.
3. Why did you **come**?

Student B to read aloud:
1. I don't think **you** understand.
2. Why did he use **that**?
3. **Should** I read it?

4 *In groups, think of the possible meanings of the word stress in the sentences below. Write a short dialog that includes all of the sentences. Perform it for the rest of the class and ask the audience to diagnose the attitude and emotion. Did they guess right?*

| It **might** be better. | Did you **give** it to her? | **Can** you help him? | We can't **run** there. |

E Read and explain

○ *Spend one minute skimming the text, and then do the paired activity below.*

Seven Easy Steps to Making a Car Insurance Claim

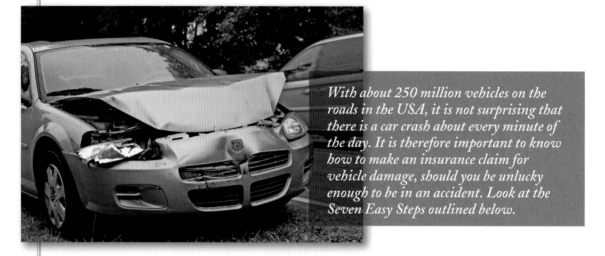

With about 250 million vehicles on the roads in the USA, it is not surprising that there is a car crash about every minute of the day. It is therefore important to know how to make an insurance claim for vehicle damage, should you be unlucky enough to be in an accident. Look at the Seven Easy Steps outlined below.

STEP 1   If there is no life-threatening injury, don't worry about calling the police right away. Remember though that you will need a police report to make the insurance claim.

STEP 2   Swap details including driver's license, insurance information, and phone numbers with the person you have collided with.

STEP 3   Get witness details and a police report to support your insurance claim. It is important for you to get in writing a record of what happened, and who was at fault, from someone who does not have a vested interest in the claim, (e.g., a witness or/and the police).

STEP 4   Contact your insurance company within 24 hours of the accident. Although the other party may be the one at fault, you should make a claim with your own insurance company. Your insurance company will be able to assist you in settling arguments with the other party over what expenses should be covered.

STEP 5   (only if the accident is the other person's fault):
Let the other party's insurance company know that you will be making a claim through your insurance company. This claim may include:
- crash insurance deductibles,
- cost of renting a car while yours is being fixed,
- loss of resale value as a result of the crash,
- time off work.
Make sure you itemize every expense!

STEP 6   Be prepared to get a call from the other insurance company asking you to explain in detail your version of the car crash. Prepare for this, because if the claim goes to court for any reason, you need to have a consistent story!

STEP 7   You may be invited to take your car directly to the insurance repair shop. If your insurance company does not have one, the insurance company adjuster will come out and estimate the damage when he/she inspects the car.

1 *Role-play these situations in pairs. Swap roles for the second situation. Explain clearly and concisely in your own words without reading directly from the text.*

    1. **Caller:** I'm out on Highway 3 and I've just collided with a truck. No one's injured, but my car is a totaled. What do I do?

        Agent: *Explain what the first steps are in making the insurance claim.*

    2. **Caller:** I had an accident last week. It wasn't my fault, and I've already filed a report, but I want to know what I can claim for, apart from the cost of the repair to my car.

        Agent: *Explain what else the claimant can ask for.*

F Intercultural matters

1 Direct answers to direct questions

> ■ A common difference between many world cultures is how direct and confrontational people are in professional situations. American customers often complain that agents from other cultures are not direct enough when answering questions. Look at this conversation:
>
> *Caller:* Why haven't I received my refund yet?
> *Agent:* At Easter time some of the people from our office go on vacation to visit their families. We're also restructuring the operations a bit.
>
> The agent's response suggests that the refund has not happened because of staff shortages. The caller may get the impression, however, that the agent is not answering frankly or taking responsibility. This may annoy the caller.
>
> ■ On the other hand, agents who sound too direct or even blame the customer will also have problems! For American customers in general, being told the truth in a frank, direct, but polite manner is important. Your job is to find the right balance for your customer.

1 *Work in pairs. Look at the caller questions below and rate the three responses in the order of appropriateness for American callers.*

    1. Why haven't I received my check yet?

        a) It must have been sent to the wrong address. .... ☐

        b) I hope to ensure you receive the check in the future. .... ☐

        c) I'll further research this and flag the unconfirmed address as a possible problem. .... ☐

    2. Why can't I use my card?

        a) If you are able to send a check for an amount that has been sent to you, we will be more than happy to help you to use your card again. .... ☐

        b) Your credit limit has been reached, and the bill is still outstanding. .... ☐

        c) You have spent too much without paying your bills. .... ☐

    3. This is completely ridiculous! Why can't you answer my question?

        a) We've lost your file. I can't answer questions without it. .... ☐

        b) If you will allow me to consult my research, I will endeavor to answer all questions asked of me. .... ☐

        c) I am not able to locate your file. Please bear with me while I search for it. .... ☐

2 *Work in small groups. Discuss these questions.*

    1. Do you think any of the responses in Activity 1 are rude?

    2. What other responses would you prefer to receive?

3 *Is American culture more direct than your culture? Discuss how can you "bridge the gap."*

4 *Respond to these sentences from the call with the appropriate directness.*

1. There's nobody else in that office that is higher up than you?

    Your culture: ....

    American culture: ....

2. This answer you are giving me is not flying.

    Your culture: ....

    American culture: ....

3. If you're sending me a check and somebody cashed it, then I need to know – I need to talk to somebody higher up!

    Your culture: ....

    American culture: ....

2 Saying *no*

- As a call center agent, you will sometimes have to refuse customer requests. It is important to make clear that it is a refusal, while remaining polite all the time. For example:
  I'm afraid that isn't something I am authorized to do.

- If your customer feels that you have agreed to do something that you did not agree to, this can cause serious problems.

- In some cultures, saying *no* is considered rude, while in others if you say *yes* when you mean *no*, your listeners will be both confused and annoyed. In American culture, a refusal in a customer service situation is expected to be apologetic but firm.

- If possible, follow your *no* with an alternative suggestion of what you are able to do. This won't always be an option, but when it is, it will help focus the customer's attention on your proactive attitude, rather than the fact that you have said *no*. For example:
  I'm sorry but that isn't possible. However I can offer …
  Unfortunately we won't be able to do that, but what we can do is …

1 *In pairs, hold a conversation on one of the topics below. Student A is unwilling to say **no** and is therefore being indirect, while Student B wants a straight answer. Swap roles and repeat. Discuss in class how you felt when you were Student B.*

1. B wants to go out after work with A, but A just wants to go straight home.
2. B wants to know A's recent quality scores, but A does not want to share this information.

2 *Work in small groups. Find direct, professional responses to the caller comments below. One person in the group will judge which response is best. Swap roles for each comment.*

1. Do you think my claim will be successful? *(You are almost certain that it won't.)*
2. What have you done with my order? *(You lost it. The customer will have to place the whole thing again.)*
3. Why am I being transferred back to the department I called originally? *(You can't deal with caller's problem. The last department misunderstood and transferred the caller to you.)*
4. When will I hear about this? I expect it to be very soon! *(You cannot commit to anything sooner than a week.)*
5. Why can't you waive the fee? I had it waived before! *(This customer has been unreliable, and no longer qualifies for fee waiving.)*
6. I want the name and direct phone number of your supervisor. *(You cannot give this information out. Your supervisor is busy and can't take the call.)*
7. Why haven't my camera repairs been done yet? *(You have no record of receiving the item for repair – it must have been lost in transit.)*
8. I want a refund for my phone bills because I didn't use my phone. *(The caller signed a contract saying that the bill is charged each month, even if the phone is not used.)*

G Role-play

○ *Work in pairs. Read the scenario and your rolecard carefully, and act out the role-play. Swap roles and repeat. After the role-play, evaluate the agent.*

Scenario

A bank customer is calling a third time about the same problem. It is important to show understanding and concern for all of the customer's concerns. The caller has lost confidence in the competence and abilities of the staff of the bank. The agent must regain the customer's trust. After each role-play evaluate the agent.

ROLECARD 1

Caller

You are the financial manager of a business company. You are calling the bank for the third time because they are still sending your statements and other communications to the old mailing address. Two other agents took your new address and told you that your details had been updated. Normally you are a patient and good-natured person, but this has made you very angry because it is affecting the business. You feel that it shouldn't take three calls to update an address, and that the other agents should be disciplined.

ROLECARD 2

Agent

You work for a bank and the caller is obviously upset and very insistent. Use active listening to let the caller know that you are aware of the problem. Remain in control of the call, and attempt to build rapport with the caller and gain his/her trust because he/she has been disappointed by your colleagues.

Evaluate the agent		
Good active listening?	YES/NO	Notes:
Did the agent control the call well?	YES/NO	Notes:
Did the apology sound sincere?	YES/NO	Why? / Why Not?
Caller satisfied/ confidence regained?	YES/NO	Why? / Why Not?

APPROPRIATE APOLOGIES

H Self-evaluation

Tasks	Check	Comments (areas for self-improvement)
A The call Did you understand the purpose of the call and detailed information, with particular reference to the caller's emotions?	☐	
B Focus on language Are you able to express regret using the third conditional or *should have done*? How about making comparisons?	☐	
C Soft skills Can you successfully respond to angry callers by apologizing and keeping control of the call? What about sounding "robotic"?	☐	
D Pronunciation Can you interpret caller attitude and emotion through word stress?	☐	
E Read and explain Can you read, synthesize, and then tell someone what you have read?	☐	
F Intercultural matters Are you able to answer direct questions politely and frankly? Are you comfortable saying *no* to customers?	☐	
G Role-play For this unit overall, what were your strengths and weaknesses?		

10 Dealing with sarcasm

What you will learn!
At the end of this unit, you will have covered:

A **The call:** listening to understand the overall purpose and details of the call, as well as the feelings of the caller

B **Focus on language:** review of conditional sentences ◆ modals with many meanings ◆ active and passive forms ◆ American idioms

C **Soft skills:** dealing with conflict

D **Pronunciation:** differentiating vowel sounds

E **Read and explain:** reading and synthesizing a story to retell to a partner in your own words

F **Intercultural matters:** women's independence ◆ multiculturalism and the American Dream

G **Role-play:** simulating a call center transaction about a credit card fraud

DAN and DORA. – DORA FINISHES HER TRAINING

GREAT! I LOVE BEING TRANSFERRED, IT'S MY NEW HOBBY!

I'M SORRY YOU HAVE BEEN TRANSFERRED SO OFTEN, BUT I ASSURE YOU THAT THIS DEPARTMENT WILL BE ABLE TO HELP YOU.

THE PERFECT WAY TO DEAL WITH SARCASM. NOW YOU DON'T NEED MY HELP ANYMORE!

WAS THAT SARCASTIC?!

A The call

1 Pre-listening activity

The caller says "Where will it end?"
What do you think the call will be about?

2 Global listening activity

 As you listen to the call for the first time, answer the questions.

1. What do you think the main purpose of the call was?
2. How were the caller and the agent feeling throughout the call?

3 Detailed listening activity

Listen to the call again. Look at the statements below and mark whether they are true (T) or false (F). Discuss your answers with the class.

1. Jane Groundling prefers to be called Ms. because she is married. .... ☐
2. The caller has talked to a supervisor previously. .... ☐
3. The caller wants the invoice to be in the company's name. .... ☐
4. The caller has already filled in a form to change the invoice name. .... ☐
5. The billing cycle is approximately every three months. .... ☐
6. Computers have been billed under the company name before. .... ☐
7. The local rep can't do anything about this problem. .... ☐
8. The caller feels confident that the next department will solve her problem. .... ☐

B Focus on language

1 Conditional sentence rules – and how to break them

1 *You have already learned the rules for conditional sentences. Test yourself by writing examples in the table below.*

Conditional type	Example
Zero	
First	
Second	
Third	

2 *Look at these unusual examples of conditional sentences. Give the meaning and explain why they break the rules. Can you find any more unusual examples in the transcript?*

Unusual conditional sentences	Meaning
If we went to the football match in the rain, we'll get really wet.	
If he goes to Tokyo next week, he'd be able to go to the conference.	
If you were going to save for that car, you would have put away at least US$10,000 by now.	

2 Modals with several functional meanings

- In this course we have looked at a number of modal verbs with different functional meanings. These may change, however, depending on the context. For example:
  You might have got one for me when you were out! I love those donuts! (You didn't get a donut. You are disapproving.)
  Would you mind opening the window? (This can be an instruction, a request, or even a suggestion.)

1 *Work in pairs. Look at the transcript and underline each modal (may, can, should, etc) statement. Write the function of each modal verb.*

3 Active and passive forms

- We often use the passive when we do not know, or do not want to say, who was responsible for the action:
  The class was canceled at the last minute.
  The invoice wasn't sent out until yesterday.

- The passive is formed with: *be* + past participle

1 *Write active and passive responses to the following caller prompts.*

1. **Caller:** My credit card was rejected at the store today!

   Agent: *You must have gone over the limit on your card. (active)*

   The limit on your card must have been reached. (passive)

2. **Caller:** Have you sent that check yet? I've been waiting for over a month!

   Agent: ....

   ....

3. **Caller:** Why isn't my internet working?

   Agent: ....

   ....

4. **Caller:** I got the check, but the amount was wrong!

   Agent: ....

   ....

2 *Work in pairs. Write a short dialog for the following scenario, using the passive and active tenses to either accuse or avoid taking responsibility.*

The caller bought a cell phone last week and thinks he/she put a charger in it that was the wrong voltage. The cell phone has not worked since. The caller wants to play down the fact that he/she connected the new phone to a high voltage charger!

The agent knows that the problems described by the caller mean that he/she most likely connected the phone to a charger or adapter of the wrong voltage. If this is true, the damage is the caller's responsibility, not the company's.

4 American idioms (3)

1 *Look at the idiomatic language in italics. Write down how you think the speaker feels each time.*

1. *This is not the first time* we've bought a computer from you people, *but I can tell you, it might be the last.*
2. *Do whatever it is you need to do,* but let me speak to your supervisor.
3. *Where will it end?*
4. *Now you're telling me* I have to …
5. *They can't do anything* locally.
6. *I get a different story every time* I call.

C Soft skills

1 Dealing with conflict

- The ideal resolution to a call that begins with conflict (as the call in this unit does) is for the agent to establish a way of working together with the caller to solve the problem.

- Once the agent has calmed the angry caller down, he/she needs to build the relationship up by working together toward a common goal. There is a lot of important functional language that will help you do this: *I can resolve this issue quickly for you though. I will update your details over the phone. You will then receive a form which you can fill out and fax back to us.*

 1 *Listen to the call again while reading the transcript. Highlight when the caller and the agent are in conflict or disagreement. Suggest possible improvements.*

Line number	Summary of conflict or disagreement		Improved agent response
		▶	
		▶	

2 *Look at the transcript and identify other words or phrases which show that the agent is working with the caller to resolve the problem.*

2 Responding to sarcasm

- Some angry or frustrated callers will tell the agent directly how they are feeling. Others may use *sarcasm* to express their feelings. Sarcasm often means saying the opposite of the true message you want to get across, with the intention of making a cutting or hurtful remark. Saying the opposite can also be called irony, but in this unit sarcasm is used for customer complaints that are expressed indirectly (for example, saying *that's fantastic* when you mean *that's awful*).

- Intonation used to express sarcasm can be very subtle. The use of sarcasm to express thoughts that are not obviously sarcastic may lead to confusion. This is especially true where there are language or cultural differences between speakers.

- It is crucial to respond to sarcastic comments as if they were a straight complaint. Do not ignore them or laugh at them. For example:

Agent: How are you today?
Caller: Well my credit card was declined – I couldn't be better!
Agent: I'm so sorry about that. It must be very frustrating for you to have no access to your credit card.

1 *Look at Unit 6 page 66 (Responding to humor) again. Then with a partner write appropriate responses to these sarcastic comments.*

1. The agent finds that the caller's problem needs a specialist and offers to transfer the call. The caller says: *Oh, I love being transferred – I've only been transferred five times today. I'm hoping to make it to ten.*

2. The caller is not very happy with the agent's communication skills and is having a hard time understanding him/her. He then says: *I love call centers. They make life so much easier!*

3. The agent has already put the caller on hold several times and asks to do it one more time. The caller says: *Go ahead. I love listening to that music – I'll sing you the song when you get back.*

2 *Choose one of the situations from Activity 1 and role-play it, using the responses you wrote. Perform your role-plays to the class and give each other feedback with the help of the form below.*

Call evaluation		
Agent skill	**Rating out of 10**	**Comments**
Dealing with conflict	_____	_____
Establishing working together	_____	_____
Responding appropriately to sarcasm	_____	_____
Caller satisfied?	_____	_____

D Pronunciation

1 Differentiating vowel sounds (2)

- To be understood by American callers it is important to pronounce vowels correctly. Consider the words *full* and *fool*. The word *fool* has a long /uː/ sound, the same vowel sound as in *rule, food, drew,* and *sue*. The word *full* has a short /ʊ/ sound, the same sound as in *foot, look, put,* and *wool*.

- The long /uː/ is a prolonged sound made with your lips rounded. The short /ʊ/ is a short sound made with your lips slightly spread.

- Another important vowel distinction is between the /æ/ and the /ɔː/ sounds in the words *can* and *con*. The /æ/ sound in *can* is the same as the one in *happy, plan,* and *ant*. The /ɔː/ sound in *con* is the same as the one in *stop, block,* and *off*.

 1 *Work in pairs. Listen to the call again and look at the transcript. Fill in the chart below with words that contain the sounds. Say the words aloud to check your answers.*

/uː/	/ʊ/	/æ/	/ɔː/

2 *Work in pairs. Sit back-to-back each with the minimal pair table below. Student A reads aloud one word from each pair. Student B listens and highlights the words. At the end check the words you highlighted. Then swap roles and repeat.*

pool	pull	shake	shock
add	odd	who'd	hood
suit	soot	pad	pod
racket	rocket	stewed	stood
Luke	look	hat	hot

3 *Work in pairs. Sit back-to-back. Read the sentences below aloud only once to your partner. Your partner closes his/her book and writes down what he/she hears. Check what your partner wrote.*

Student A
1. We would put the books next to the boots.
2. You should look at it often.
3. Sue is a woman who looks odd in autumn.

Student B
1. At last he stopped to attend a fall concert.
2. The truth could offend Luke and Anne.
3. He took a good look at Alice.

E Read and explain

○ *Spend one minute skiming either Text A or Text B. Then take turns to retell your story to your partner. Use your own words and don't read directly from the text.*

✦✦✦ Text A ✦✦✦

THE END OF THE LINE

I had been out of work, but looking for employment, for about eight weeks when I decided to go into the local Job Center and talk to someone about making an appointment to register for unemployment benefits, and also to access a job-seeking skills program. When I went into the Job Center, a grumpy elderly lady said I would have to go home and phone to make an appointment. I complained that every time I phoned, I got put on hold, and the music drove me crazy. But she refused to budge. I protested further, and the only concession she made was to offer to call me instead. As soon as I left the building, I got a phone call, and I agreed I would go into the Job Center for my appointment the following week, which I duly did. I registered my claim. After hearing by mail that this had been successful, I then phoned to say I would like to enroll in a job-seeking course. They said I couldn't make an appointment for this over the phone – I would need to come to the Job Center in person and fill in an application personally … and no, this couldn't be done online! So I went in the following day and filled out a course registration form to attend a course entitled Customer Service Made Easy. The irony of this did not escape me!

✦✦✦ Text B ✦✦✦

WILD FIRE RAGE

A couple of months ago I was working away in my suburban office on the outskirts of San Francisco when, from my office window, I noticed a suspicious curl of smoke that could spell disaster in our dry and drought-stricken suburb. When I looked further it seemed that the fire was coming from a trash can outside the low-rise apartment building opposite. As a responsible citizen, I called the Facilities Management Office for the apartment building. After ten minutes of taking my details, I told them that there was a fire in the trash can outside their building. They suggested I could do one of two things: either call the fire department immediately, or fill in a request for service online. The request online, I was assured, would be activated within five working days. The call ended with: "Have a good day." What did I choose? Neither. Instead I went over to the sink in my pantry, filled a small bucket with water, crossed the road, and put out the fire.

F Intercultural matters

1 Women's independence

■ Women are addressed in formal situations differently in different countries. The caller in this call asks the agent to call her *Ms*. This title means that her marital status is not revealed. (*Mrs.* means she is married; *Miss* means she is not.) For some women this is a statement of independence because they are not defined by marriage.

■ Women's independence is an important part of Western culture (particularly American culture). In the past, American women fought for the right to have careers with as many opportunities as men, rather than being tied to looking after the children.

1 *Work in pairs. Look at the statements below and decide whether they are true (T) or false (F) for American culture and your culture.*

Your culture	American culture	
☐	☐	1. Single mothers are an accepted part of society.
☐	☐	2. It is acceptable for a woman to have children by different men without getting married.
☐	☐	3. Most women keep their father's surname even when they are married.
☐	☐	4. It is acceptable for women to decide not to have children or get married.
☐	☐	5. Women often pursue careers and reach top leadership positions.
☐	☐	6. Women frequently work when they are pregnant and/or have young children.
☐	☐	7. Married couples usually have joint bank accounts, which they both have equal access to.
☐	☐	8. Women can be the main income earner in the household.

2 *Work in groups. Discuss your answers to Activity 1. Note down values that you think are of high importance (core values) and of low importance (non-core values) for American women. Which ones are shared with women in your culture?*

Core values	Shared or different?

Non-core values	Shared or different?

2 Multiculturalism and the American Dream

■ The American Dream is fulfilled when a man or woman from a simple background rises to a high position and is extremely successful. The idea behind it is that you can succeed no matter what your origins. The dream grew from the roots of American society: immigrants from all over the world were given a "new start," and were successful because of their will to succeed – unlike in other countries where established class systems would have given them no chance. This is why the U.S. is known as the "land of opportunity."

1 *Compare your country with the United States in terms of demographics and diversity. Use the information below to make a poster of the similarities and differences. Present it to the rest of the group.*

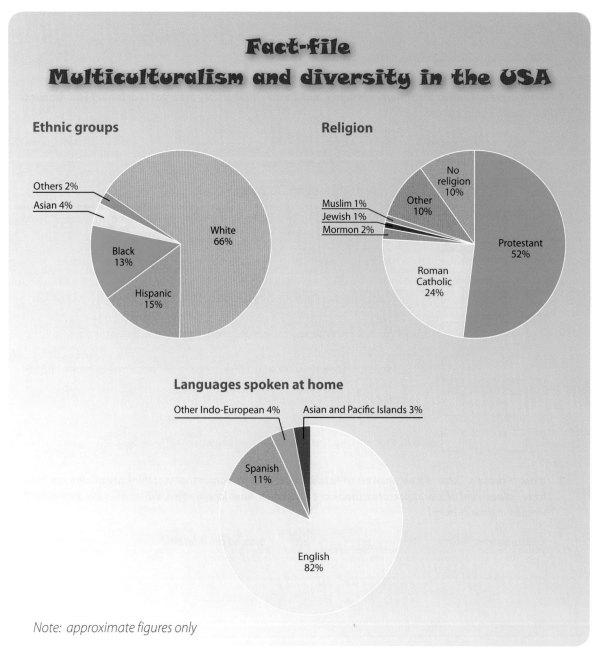

Note: *approximate figures only*

2 *Work in pairs. Using the information you have learned in this and other units, brainstorm five ways in which your life might be different if you lived in the United States. Think particularly about the role of women and general career opportunities.*

3 *In the same pairs, create a role-play in which you show three key differences between your culture and American culture. You can use topics from previous* Intercultural matters *sections, such as retirement, education, and family. The role-play should demonstrate how to bridge the gap between the two cultures. Present your role-play to the class.*

G Role-play

○ *Work in pairs. Read the scenario and your rolecard, then act out the role-play. Swap roles and repeat. Each time decide if the agent successfully apologized and guided the caller in reporting the fraud.*

Scenario

A very angry and frustrated caller is contacting the credit card company's Customer Service Department. The caller has been trying to get some information about credit card fraud because some expenses which cannot be explained have appeared on his/her latest statement. The caller is convinced that someone has been using his/her credit card and that the bank has been slow in taking action. The caller has called before and claims that no action has been taken yet. The caller is threatening to report the incident to the authorities.

ROLECARD I

Caller

You are a wealthy consumer and you love to shop. You always use your credit card, but you noticed on your statement from two months ago that some charges were not yours. You immediately called your bank. They said they would block your card and investigate the matter. You are now calling the bank again because your card wasn't blocked and more unexplained charges have appeared on your account. You are extremely upset and want the card to be blocked as soon as possible. If the agent does not do as you wish, you should use sarcasm to make your point.

ROLECARD 2

Agent

You are dealing with an angry caller. You must be very attentive to what he/she says and you must:

- find out what the caller's concern is,
- empathize and apologize,
- regain the caller's trust,
- tell the caller that fraud cases must be reported in writing as per company policy.

Evaluate the agent		
Good active listening?	YES/NO	Notes:
Did the agent show empathy?	YES/NO	Notes:
Did the apology sound sincere?	YES/NO	Why? / Why Not?
Caller satisfied/ confidence regained?	YES/NO	Why? / Why Not?

H Self-evaluation

Tasks	Check	Comments (areas for self-improvement)
A The call Did you understand the purpose of the call and detailed information, with particular reference to the caller's emotions?	☐	
B Focus on language Do you feel confident about using different kinds of conditional sentences? How about modal verbs and their different functions? Do you understand the reasons for using the passive rather than the active form?	☐	
C Soft skills Are you confident that you can deal with conflict in a suitable way?	☐	
D Pronunciation Can you differentiate between different vowel sounds?	☐	
E Read and explain Can you read, synthesize, and then tell someone what you have read?	☐	
F Intercultural matters Can you use your knowledge of American attitudes to women's independence and the American Dream to bridge the gap between cultures?	☐	
G Role-play For this unit overall, what were your strengths and weaknesses?		

Notes

Notes

Notes

Audio CD track listing

Track	Unit	Length
1	Introduction	0'09"
2	Unit 1 The call	3'50"
3	Unit 1 D3 Additional Listening	0'49"
4	Unit 2 The call	4'57"
5	Unit 2 D1 Additional Listening	0'28"
6	Unit 3 The call	6'26"
7	Unit 3 D1 Additional Listening	0'29"
8	Unit 4 The call	4'31"
9	Unit 4 D1 Additional Listening	0'33"
10	Unit 5 The call	6'14"
11	Unit 5 D1 Additional Listening (1)	0'42"
12	Unit 5 D1 Additional Listening (2)	0'18"
13	Unit 6 The call	7'44"
14	Unit 6 D1 Additional Listening	0'21"
15	Unit 7 The call	8'16"
16	Unit 8 The call	6'38"
17	Unit 8 D1 Additional Listening (1)	0'39"
18	Unit 8 D1 Additional Listening (2)	0'32"
19	Unit 9 The call	8'41"
20	Unit 10 The call	6'38"

Audio transcripts are in the accompanying booklet.

Acknowledgments

Layout and design: Transnet Pte Ltd, Singapore
based on an original design by: werkstatt für gebrauchsgrafik, Berlin

Cover design: Studioleng, Singapore

Call center agents: Photography by Samuel Rosales & Winston Baltasar, VISTA DIGITAL PRODUCTION, Manila

Cartoon illustrations: Oxford Designers & Illustrators, Oxford

Other photos and illustrations: p. 9 ©iStockphoto.com/molotovcoketail; p. 10 Tan Kok Yong; p. 21 *(top left)* ©iStockphoto.com/RiverNorthPhotography; *(top right)* ©iStockphoto.com/corfoto; *(bottom)* ©iStockphoto.com/ChuckSchugPhotography; p. 30 LiDan Illustration & Design Studio; p. 41 Tan Kok Yong; p. 53 *(top)* ©iStockphoto.com/yekorzh; *(middle)* ©iStockphoto.com/NickS; *(bottom left)* ©iStockphoto.com/Rouzes; *(bottom right)* ©iStockphoto.com/micsell; p. 55 ©iStockphoto.com/sjlocke; p. 65 ©iStockphoto.com/killerb10; p. 75 ©iStockphoto.com/davincidig; p. 76 ©iStockphoto.com/jacomstephens; p. 77 ©iStockphoto.com/compucow

Sound recordings for audio CD: Anzak Modern Music Productions, Manila

CONTACT US!
COURSEBOOK TRANSCRIPT

UNIT 1

AGENT: Thank you for calling Atlantic Aroma Coffee Center. We are here to provide you excellent customer service. My name is Rajiv. How can I assist you?

5 **CALLER:** I'm wanting to find out about um information on a franchise opportunity. You know, I've always wanted to open an Atlantic coffee shop, and I love the way you guys do things.

AGENT: OK, I am pleased to hear that. So do you
10 want to open a coffee shop [Yes.] or you already have one, and you just want to brand it Atlantic?

CALLER: Exactly. That's exactly right – the second.

AGENT: OK, well the way it works is that we have
15 to take down your information, we email you a template, and you have to fill out and then fax it to another number at the top, and then the rep contacts you within seven days.

CALLER: OK.

20 **AGENT:** OK, you wanna do that? [Yes, OK.] OK, so what is your last name?

CALLER: Ah, last name is Green. G-R-E-E-N.

AGENT: And your first name?

CALLER: Ashley. A-S-H-L-E-Y

25 **AGENT:** And your phone number?

CALLER: It's area 573 uh 692-6218.

AGENT: Thank you. And your email address?

CALLER: A-S-H dot 34 at yahoo.com.

AGENT: All right, I'll repeat that to you: it is A-S-H
30 dot 34 at yahoo.com. [That's correct.] Thank you, Ms. Green. What is your mailing address?

CALLER: 273 [uh-huh] Rockport Ave [Uh-huh.] Sheldon [S-H-E-L-D-O-N?] Exactly. [All right.] Missouri, MO [Mmm-hmmm.] 65109 [Thank you.]
35 No, I'm sorry. Let me redo the zip code: 65020.

AGENT: Can I just put you on hold for a second?

CALLER: Sure, no problem.

AGENT: All right, thank you for holding. OK, I'm processing the request right now.

40 **CALLER:** All right. Will I get the email immediately?

AGENT: Yes uh yeah, that is what I'm doing right now.

CALLER: OK. Great.

45 **AGENT:** Yes, so just bear with me a sec. And by the time I finish this you should have it. All right, that has been sent out to you.

CALLER: OK, um let me ask you. Is there a website you could direct me to that'd give some
50 information on the franchising? I mean I don't know anything much about this idea … it may be a crazy one!

AGENT: Uh-hmm a website … no, as far as franchising, no. We do have one for sales, but um
55 as far as franchising contracts and stuff like that, you'll have to wait for a rep from that part of the country to contact you. It takes normally seven business days from the date that you submit your form.

60 **CALLER:** OK.

AGENT: You get it?

CALLER: Uh, I'm going to check right now … Got it. Thank you.

AGENT: Did you want a request number for
65 today, like a confirmation number?

CALLER: Um, is that necessary?

AGENT: No, it is just a confirmation that you called in.

CALLER: No, I don't think so. So … well the next
70 step is that a rep will call me?

AGENT: Yes, in about a week, a rep will make contact.

CALLER: Like what kind of things do they want to know.

75 **AGENT:** Well, it's really just introductory … get a feel, you know about how much you know about what you're getting yourself into. You seem a bit of an old hand at this, you know … if you have your own shop already … like, when did you
80 open it?

CALLER: Last year … only last year, but I'm retired now and and I used to run another business … and I got sick of all the lunches with the girls, you know.

85 **AGENT:** OK, that's great … uh there's the other thing the rep checks out … you know, whether you have a business head. But you know you sound perfect for this. Is there anything else I can help you with at this stage?

90 **CALLER:** No, that's fine. You've been very helpful.

AGENT: Well, if there isn't anything else, Ms. Green, thank you for calling Atlantic today.

95 **CALLER:** Thank you. Bye.

AGENT: Thank you again and have a good day!

Additional Listening D3

Arkansas, California, Connecticut, Florida, Georgia, Illinois, Louisiana, Massachusetts, Michigan, Mississippi, Missouri, New Jersey, New York, North Dakota, Ohio, Pennsylvania, Tennessee, Texas, Virginia, Wisconsin

UNIT 2

AGENT: Thank you for calling Pet Fix. This is Shelley. How may I help you today?

CALLER: Oh, hi, I'm ringing up from Denver and I'm … I'm just inquiring [Colorado?] Yes in Colorado. You see there are a lot of
5 cattle here. I've got a herd of more than 50 and there are cattle that are coming down with colic, which is real bad 'cause they're dying from it, and the vet told us to use uh Colixin powder. I just came back from seeing him, and he says
10 Colixin should fix them.

AGENT: Umm … OK … How can I help you?

CALLER: I'm trying to find out, can we buy it in bulk?

AGENT: Can you buy it in bulk? OK. Do you have
15 a store, or is it only for personal?

CALLER: Huh? Er it's for the cattle …

AGENT: Oh, for the cattle … OK.

CALLER: What's happening is a lot of cattle, because of the drought, there's uh no grass
20 around, and they're eating and chewing up uh the dirt from the ground. Blocking up their stomachs, and we've had a couple of cattle die from it last week. This is what we're going through.

AGENT: OK.

25 **CALLER:** Yes, and the vets are telling us to use Colixin powder.

AGENT: OK.

CALLER: We're going to use one cup a week or one cup every two weeks. Now, as I said, in my
30 herd we've got over 50, and we're going to use it on all of them. I wonder if we can get it in bulk? And how big? And how much?

AGENT: OK. Are you able to hold for a moment? I'll just check some information about this.

35 **CALLER:** Sure.

AGENT: OK.

AGENT: Hello?

CALLER: Yeah?

AGENT: OK. Thank you very much for waiting.
40 OK, with regard to this, you can only buy the Colixin product from our main outlets on the stock list. OK?

CALLER: But where … where are they?

AGENT: OK, do you have a paper and pen with
45 you? I'll give you a list of our major outlets on the stock list where you can –

CALLER: Yeah, OK, uh but um in bulk?

AGENT: Um … you'll need to talk to them about that, but um OK.

50 **CALLER:** Oops, sorry about that.

AGENT: OK, yes, so here's the … do you have a paper and pen handy?

CALLER: Yeah, go for it. Is this somebody in Denver?

55 **AGENT:** OK. So I'll just give you the list of our outlets on the stock list in Colorado. OK?

CALLER: Well, that's no good, 'cause I can't travel very far right now to pick up Coloxin. I need somebody right here in Denver. I can't leave the
60 herd to pick up Colixin. I need someone in Denver. And if not, can I speak to the managing director about getting a bulk order because we need 60, 80, about 100 pounds of that stuff, and I'm not paying for 20-ounce jars.

65 **AGENT:** OK. So um … with regard to this, we only have the list of our major outlets, and we don't have information about the bulk purchase. You'll need to … mmm OK we … only give the outlet list from our major stock list … so you can inquire
70 about purchasing bulk.

CALLER: OK, so, in Denver is there anybody?

AGENT: OK mm so you can go to Health Mart Plus, and there's also a Pet Mart listed.

CALLER: Oh, yeah … but they don't do bulk.
75 No, no … look, don't you package it there? Isn't it … aren't … aren't I in the place where they package this stuff?

AGENT: OK, because, well … with regard to this … um … I mean buying it in bulk, you –

80 **CALLER:** Yeah, but is it still … uh it should still be in 20-ounce containers at those places, or even 10, 15-ounce containers. Hmm. I want to buy a real big box of this stuff … you know, you know – loose … that we actually get in pounds for these
85 cattle.

AGENT: I'm sorry, but we don't do that; we don't have any larger sizes here um … there are only the ones that are on the market.

CALLER: OK. Can I speak to your supervisor then?
90 Please, because you must be able to get it straight

from the factory before they package it up and get it from there and put it in a big bag or a big box. That's what the vet said to ask. You know what I mean? I don't wanna mess around with small amounts. Waste of time.

AGENT: But we don't do that actually; it's a company policy. We don't sell it in bulk, but I'll forward you … your … your interest on that size, but um as of now, we don't do that.

100 **CALLER:** That's ridiculous. Is there a managing director of the company or somebody that I can contact about this?

AGENT: OK, wait for a moment. Are you able to hold for a moment? I'll ask my supervisor.

105 **CALLER:** All right, thank you.

AGENT: Hello? Yes, thank you so much for waiting. With regard to that inquiry, I've already consulted my supervisor about that and we don't … mmm we don't have any … mmm you can just
110 talk to the store manager about that because uh we have agreed … we have an … we have an agreement with our distributors that … um … we can only … our consumers can only purchase our products from them. OK? So we really don't um
115 directly sell to our consumers. Even if uh-mm you want to buy it in bulk, you need to buy it from our distributors.

CALLER: Yeah, that's crazy! OK … all right … we'll go to another company. Thank you, bye.

120 **AGENT:** Bye.

Additional Listening D1

it's	we've	you'll
there's	we'll	aren't
they're	I'll	that's

UNIT 3

AGENT: Thank you for calling Fast Phones. My name is Greg. How may I help you?

CALLER: Hi. I need my phone number changed.

AGENT: OK, I'll be happy to change your number.
5 But may I ask you if this also changes the area code of your number? Or just the number?

CALLER: No, number.

AGENT: Just the number being changed?

CALLER: Yes.

10 **AGENT:** OK, ma'am. No problem. May I ask also, are you using your Fast Phone to call me right now?

CALLER: No.

AGENT: OK, good. Because after we change your
15 number, I'm gonna guide you to activating your phone with your new number. OK? May I please have your cell phone number?

CALLER: 615-715-0470. OK. Hang on, the elevator is here …

20 **AGENT:** I'm sorry, you're breaking up a little bit. If you're in an elevator, you break up.

CALLER: Sorry.

AGENT: That's OK. Let me see if I got your number correctly. You said 615-715-0470?

25 **CALLER:** Yes.

AGENT: Thank you very much. May I have your name please?

CALLER: Mimi Garcia.

AGENT: Thank you very much. And your
30 password, please?

CALLER: Sweetie pie.

AGENT: Thank you very much. I'm gonna take a look then. Stay on the line, OK? Just while I access your account. Give me some more time, OK? I'm
35 just preparing the account to do the number change, OK?

CALLER: OK.

AGENT: May I know why you want to change your number?

40 **CALLER:** Ah, 'cause I don't want people to have it.

AGENT: Oh, I see. OK, I do understand that.

CALLER: Do you guys charge for a private number?

45 **AGENT:** You mean like a caller-ID doesn't appear with your number?

CALLER: Yes.

AGENT: Mmm. OK, you have to request actually for that. Ah, like a caller-ID block. So I'll be
50 connecting your call to technical support after to um … do a caller-ID block, OK?

CALLER: Oh, no. That's fine. I was just asking.

AGENT: Anyway, you can also do this on a certain number you call, if you're gonna do um … a caller-
55 ID block. It's by pressing 451. Or if you want to override that caller-ID block, you just press 428 and then the number, OK?

CALLER: OK.

AGENT: OK, so that's an option that you can do by
60 yourself. Now, give me a couple of minutes more; let me prepare your line to change the number, OK?

CALLER: OK.

AGENT: Give me a couple of minutes more.

65 **CALLER:** I don't want anyone else to have it.

AGENT: I'm requesting a number now. Um, you might want to have a pen … a pen and a paper to write down your new number, OK? The area code is still gonna be the same. It's 615, right? OK. This
70 is gonna be the number: 615-300-8358.

CALLER: OK.

AGENT: I think that's a very easy number to remember, isn't it? Um … let me just register this number, change your old number now, OK? Stay
75 on the line.

CALLER: OK.

AGENT: Now, I'm gonna guide you through the programming steps. Now, you're still using the uh Quatro Phone right?

80 **CALLER:** Yes.

AGENT: OK then. I'm gonna get my programming tools ready. I want you to turn on your Quatro Fast Phone.

CALLER: OK.

85 **AGENT:** And if it starts to show the date or the time, just tell me, OK?

CALLER: OK.

AGENT: It's showing now?

CALLER: Yes.

90 **AGENT:** Good. I need you to tap the hash key twice. Or do you have the tone, uh the uh dial pad in front of you already?

CALLER: Yes.

AGENT: OK, good.

95 **CALLER:** Twice?

AGENT: Yes, tap it twice, and then type this number in: 1314, then 33.

CALLER: OK.

AGENT: Now then, another hash sign after,
100 please.

CALLER: OK.

AGENT: Now there's gonna be an added dialog box. I want you to tap that please. And this'll highlight your number, your cell phone number
105 field, right?

CALLER: Yes.

AGENT: I want you to enter your new number there. It's 615-300-8358.

CALLER: OK.

110 **AGENT:** Now, do you see an MS ID field?

CALLER: Yes.

AGENT: I want you to tap on that line and enter your old Fast Phone cell phone number.

CALLER: The old one?

115 **AGENT:** Or do you still have the old one there? Do you still see it?

CALLER: Yeah.

AGENT: OK, good. Just leave it as it is. OK, um the MS ID should be the old number still as of now.
120 OK?

CALLER: OK.

AGENT: Now, after you do that … OK … I want you to press space, on the space dialog box.

CALLER: OK.

125 **AGENT:** Then what you do is say something like "Congratulations" … you know, something like that, right?

CALLER: OK.

AGENT: Good. I want you to tap "OK" on that
130 then.

CALLER: OK.

AGENT: Now leave that phone a bit for four hours for the programming to work. So don't touch anything, huh? Now, you need to leave that
135 phone, but if you want to put it on charger, then please do. OK?

CALLER: OK.

AGENT: But more than anything else, just don't touch anything on that phone, OK?

140 **CALLER:** OK.

AGENT: OK then. Let me just give you a quick recap. I was able to change your number. Just remember your new number is 615-300-8358, OK?

145 **CALLER:** Yes.

AGENT: OK, then. Is there anything else I can assist you with tonight?

CALLER: That's it.

AGENT: May I ask, are you satisfied with the level
150 of service I've provided you tonight?

CALLER: Yes.

AGENT: Great. Oh, another thing I'd like to inform you of is that you have an account spending limit, OK? Of $125. And your running balance right now
155 is $120. You're 80% closer already. Please don't do any extra usage that'll "tip" you over. You know if you go over, it cuts out the service, OK? Your bill balance is $123.35, OK? Please don't do any extra usage that might uh "tip" you over and have some
160 service disruption. You could make some partial payments right now, that would even be better.

CALLER: OK, thank you.

AGENT: You're very welcome. I appreciate you allowing me to assist you tonight. And thank you
165 for choosing Fast Phones. Have a great evening now, OK?

CALLER: All right, bye.

AGENT: Bye now. You take care, OK?

Additional Listening D1

1. I don't believe I said for you to do that!
2. Who asked for that to be done?
3. Can't you see it there in the account details?
4. This is simply unacceptable.
5. I thought that I was getting a full refund a month ago? You've always said that I was.
6. Never mind that now. Let me speak to a supervisor immediately!

UNIT 4

AGENT: Welcome to Western Finance. My name is Isabelle Red. May I have your loan number, please?

CALLER: The number is 968 059 687.

5 **AGENT:** OK, and may I know who am I speaking with, please?

CALLER: My name is Kenny Smithson.

AGENT: OK, and Kenny, can I call you Kenny? [Yeah sure.] I need you to verify the last four digits
10 of your Security number.

CALLER: This uh 5674.

AGENT: OK, that's confirmed. May I have your home address and your home phone number?

CALLER: Hmm uh … home phone number is
15 uh … 342-5745.

AGENT: And?

CALLER: But my cell phone numbers, I don't know, you might have different numbers 'cause I've changed around, you know. How about 987-
20 654-321?

AGENT: Yes, we have, can I just confirm 987-654-321. OK, how about your mailing address?

CALLER: Mailing address, P.O. Box 56743, Bluepoint Beach, Florida, 456132.

25 **AGENT:** That's P.O. Box 56743? [No, last digit 3.] and zip code 456132? Correct.

CALLER: You really need to know your numbers in your game, don't you?

AGENT: That's for sure! OK, thank you for
30 providing me that information. And how can I help you today?

CALLER: Um, I've just received my last payment here. There's a miscellaneous fee for $15. There shouldn't be anything extra on this bill payment.
35 Can you tell me what that is, please?

AGENT: Um … hmm, so apart from the miscellaneous fee of $15, is there anything else that I can assist you with?

CALLER: Sorry, I didn't hear the last thing you
40 said.

AGENT: So it's just finding out about the $15, right?

CALLER: Right.

AGENT: I'll need to put you on hold for a minute.
45 Is that OK?

CALLER: Uh sure, all right.

AGENT: Thank you for patiently waiting. Hello? Kenny?

CALLER: Yep.

50 **AGENT:** I need to transfer your call to our Collections Department for them to be able to give you the uh explanation of your excess 15-dollar fee. Is that OK?

CALLER: All right. Collection Department. Why
55 the Collection Department?

AGENT: I'm really not sure why this amount has been billed. Don't worry, they'll sort it out.

CALLER: Do you think this is a regular amount to be billed, or just uh …?

60 **AGENT:** No. It's probably just a one-time … one-time payment. Yes, it must be something minor like that, I suppose.

CALLER: A one-time payment?

AGENT: Yes. OK, just in case we miss this
65 connection, here's the number.

CALLER: I'm sorry, uh, what's your name again?

AGENT: My name is Isabelle.

CALLER: Isabelle. And you can't answer my question?

70 **AGENT:** OK … I can only confirm with you that there was a 15-dollar amount here … for this account, but I wouldn't … uh I'm not able to provide you with why there was an excess 15-dollar fee.

75 **CALLER:** There! So what you're saying is … there was $15 but you're not able to explain it to me.

AGENT: I'm afraid I don't know. It's likely to be something small, like an underpayment one
80 month that has just shown up. Yes, it must be something like that.

5

CALLER: Uh … OK uh your customer service is strange here. Like you're not connected that much. OK, Isabelle, what was that phone number?

85

AGENT: OK … here … that's 564-72-920.

CALLER: 920 … Isabelle … uh I mean I don't like that I'm getting transferred to another call … that I might get dropped off um … You've been really helpful, and I don't think its right to waste time and all this inefficiency.

90

AGENT: OK, yes, I understand.

CALLER: I wonder if I can speak to your supervisor, please?

95

AGENT: OK, so you would like to talk to the supervisor instead of Collections?

CALLER: Yes!

AGENT: Before I transfer your call, uh is there anything else that I can assist you with?

100

CALLER: Are you transferring me to your supervisor?

AGENT: Yes.

CALLER: OK, what's your supervisor's name?

AGENT: I apologize, I don't know his name, but you'll be looked after, don't worry. That's again the 15-dollars fee, right? You don't like talking to so many people about it. Is that the problem?

105

CALLER: Yes, ma'am. And Isabelle, I mean, I'm trying to be patient myself here, you know, be courteous, all of that.

110

AGENT: Yes.

CALLER: It just seems like strange customer service from the company. You should be able to give me one-stop service, don't you think?

115

AGENT: Sure. OK. Anyway, I'll be transferring your call now.

Additional Listening D1

1. You've been very helpful.
2. The instructions were really clear.
3. Thank you for your time and effort.
4. I am thrilled that this was done the way it was.
5. I appreciate you letting me know so soon.
6. Are all of the other agents as knowledgeable as you are?

UNIT 5

AGENT: Thank you for calling CameraSnap Company. This is Anne. How can I help you today?

5

CALLER: Uh, I called a couple of weeks ago, now I guess I'm gonna get … uh I'm gonna send my camera in.

AGENT: Um … uh-huh … OK … um.

CALLER: See … uh. [Uh-huh.] And I got an email with the authorization number.

10

AGENT: Return authorization number? OK?

CALLER: And the information, my … uh do I need to send in my battery charger and all the stuff in with it?

AGENT: OK, I see. Can I have the first …

15 the … return authorization number that you have?

CALLER: 567-83-468.

AGENT: 567-83-468. OK, just a moment. Is your name Gary Sharpe?

20

CALLER: Yes.

AGENT: OK, and phone number is 789-4763?

CALLER: Right.

AGENT: Right. Let me just go on over your record here … just give me a minute … I'm just trying to

25 read the record … OK. So your camera won't turn on, OK. What charger are you using? A Rapid? Are you using a Rapid Charger?

CALLER: Uh no, actually it's a … an Battpack Ultraenergy.

30

AGENT: Oh, I see. OK. You just need to send the camera itself without any batteries, without any memory card, and without any charger, OK?

CALLER: Don't send any other stuff?

AGENT: No, no, no accessories, OK? So you just

35 send the camera itself.

CALLER: OK.

AGENT: All right? Are you clear now?

CALLER: Yeah, when will I know what's up with it?

40

AGENT: Um not sure … Um you said that the camera was … has been dropped, right? And –

CALLER: No, no, no, I didn't, uh not to my knowledge anyway. I was heading out of town

45 in the car, and it was on the seat and it started beeping. [OK. I see.] And it wouldn't uh, wouldn't turn on, and er –

AGENT: Oh, I've … I … yes … yes … my mistake … um … hmm … yes, my mistake uh

50 I thought it was said here it was dropped. It wasn't … it wasn't sorry um hmm –

CALLER: No, I I've taken very good care of it. I was gonna give it to my son. He's coming home from college for a few days, and I wanted to give him a

55 camera that works [Yes, of course.] so he can send back pictures. Looking at it now, it's stuck open with the lens sticking out and I don't know if that means anything?

AGENT: You're using a rechargeable Ultraenergy
60   battery?

CALLER: Right.

AGENT: Double A. Aside from those Double A
batteries, have you tried other types of batteries,
such as lithium?

65   **CALLER:** Yeah, I've tried some regular Double
A's.

AGENT: Double A?

CALLER: Yeah, I know … uh … they should
be –

70   **AGENT:** You know, uh Gary, I would strongly
suggest that you use lithium batteries, especially
lithium batteries, before you send your camera for
repair, just to avoid any battery issue. All right? Or
else it'll just be wasting our time and effort when
75   after uh realizing that it's a battery issue, the repair
center will tell you off, because you cannot send
ba … uh Ultraenergy rechargeable batteries, and
we don't recommend just Double A battery. We
uh we only recommend lithium battery pack. OK?
80   So, um you know –

CALLER: Double A's are not recommended? I
thought … uh that's why I bought this thing, so
it wouldn't be too expensive on upkeep. It said
recommended [Uh not … not Double A.] is to use
85   rechargeable batteries.

AGENT: Yes, yes, rechargeable batteries are fine.
Just that it has to be lithium. But we're not sure if
it … if it has something to do with the charger that
you're using or the Ultraenergy batteries itself. I'm
90   not very sure, so I would strongly suggest that you
try first to use lithium batteries regardless of the
brands. OK? Lithium batteries, before you send –

CALLER: Lithium, not uh –

AGENT: Not alkaline batteries, not Double A
95   batteries. OK? So lithium, lithium batteries, just to
be sure.

CALLER: What kind of uh … it's not Double A, it
takes Double A –

AGENT: You can –

100   **CALLER:** Somehow uh like uh CameraSnap
battery.

AGENT: Um well … I … uh, of course, I would
suggest CameraSnap, but it's regardless of the
brands of the batteries, as long as it's lithium,
105   even if it's Double A batteries, or even it's the CS
Lithium batteries.

CALLER: CS, that's the CameraSnap, yeah?

AGENT: Uh … yes, you can also try … uh to
find … other … Longmax lithium batteries,
110   regardless of the brand. You're not … we're not
the only one.

CALLER: You can buy uh you can buy a lithium
battery so it just looks like a Double A, right?

AGENT: Yeah yeah, you can do that. Just make
115   sure it's lithium, OK? You know I made the exact
same mistake. I was using the wrong batteries and
I had a similar problem.

CALLER: All right.

AGENT: And as a piece of advice, just make sure
120   that you clean the uh battery compartment of the
camera. Clean using a dry cloth uh to try to reach
the uh battery context, and then –

CALLER: Is that at the bottom?

AGENT: Yes, yes. And then –

125   **CALLER:** Can you uh want a stick uh cotton down
in there or something?

AGENT: Uh … just uh try to … just try to reach
the battery compartment, the uh compartment,
just … just don't use any … wet material or wet
130   cloth … just a dry cloth.

CALLER: No alcohol or anything? I was using
alcohol before.

AGENT: No alcohol. No, definitely no alcohol, no
liquid, OK?

135   **CALLER:** Right, OK!

AGENT: OK, just try that first, it's … I'm not very
sure, but sometimes it really works. Believe me,
OK?

CALLER: OK, if that does not work, just send it in?

140   **AGENT:** Yes, if the cleaning and the lithium
battery really don't work, even with the using of
lithium batteries, then just send your camera in for
repair. OK?

CALLER: All right. Do I need to send this
145   Ultraenergy thing in, or just the camera?

AGENT: Just the camera itself.

CALLER: I don't send anything else?

AGENT: Yes, nothing else.

CALLER: Was this uh … this email says for power
150   issue, send all batteries being used, adaptors,
memory card, chargers –

AGENT: Yes. But um … if that is uh … if you're
using a CameraSnap rechargeable battery or
charger … because that is … and then we could
155   also try to, you know, fix if it has something to do
with the charger, CameraSnap charger, but since
you're using an Ultraenergy, we cannot try to fix
it … that one, OK?

CALLER: OK. Sure it's straightforward what I have
160   to do now.

AGENT: All right? So I think we're all set now?

CALLER: OK.

AGENT: All right. Good luck and so thank you
for calling CameraSnap. Have a nice day, Gary.
165   Bye-bye.

CALLER: Bye. Thank you.

AGENT: Welcome.

CALLER: Bye.

Additional Listening D1 (1)

1. The meeting ran late this morning.
2. I haven't seen him since last week.
3. What is her husband doing at the office? He should be at home.
4. Can you hold for just a moment? I won't be long.
5. I think that he would become the most valuable employee.
6. Could you send that document to him today, please?
7. The hotel burned down last summer.
8. We have never spent our vacation near home.

Additional Listening D1 (2)

vegetable	actually	separate
worsening	automatically	primary

UNIT 6

AGENT: Thank you for calling Fast Phones. This is Ally. How can I help you today?

CALLER: Yes um ... my husband and I both have phones and ... and we are supposed to share 800
5 "anytime" minutes, and they're saying that we went over already ... and we ... well ... he only used 51 minutes ... and I think ... oh well, there was some deal where when you're calling nights and weekends and cell phone to cell phone and
10 that's supposed to be free.

AGENT: Oh, I understand that, ma'am. So right now you have two phones that are sharing 800 minutes, and they're saying you already went over it? Is that right?

15 CALLER: Yes, ma'am.

AGENT: Let me go ahead and check. May I have your ... Fast Phone number please?

CALLER: Oh, just wait a sec ... all right 527-81-479.

20 AGENT: Thank you, ma'am, and may I have your name please?

CALLER: Amy Bradley.

AGENT: And Ms. Bradley, may I also have the name of the account and the password please?

25 CALLER: The name of the account is my ... my name: Amy Bradley.

AGENT: Oh, all right. Thank you, Ms. Bradley. What about the password or the last four digits of your Social ... of your Social, ma'am?

30 CALLER: 6572.

AGENT: Oh, all right. Thank you, Ms. Bradley. Give me a moment while I review the account and let me see what happened, OK?

CALLER: OK.

35 AGENT: All right, did you check it ... out through the website, Ms. Bradley?

CALLER: Ma'am?

AGENT: Where did you check, I mean the minutes usage, and ... where they're saying you went
40 over?

CALLER: Oh, no. On the phone.

AGENT: Oh, on the phone. Let me see. And that it showed you that you used about 51 minutes only, but ... but then it also says you went over. Is that
45 correct?

CALLER: Yeah, it says we owe 109, and we got zero minutes left. He's over one minute. And the way they add it up, I think they're adding to the ... um ... all the nights and weekends ... and
50 the cell phone to cell phone ... like when he calls me. It was supposed to be 800 ... and with one phone, they're saying it's over. They shouldn't be billing that amount in my view.

AGENT: Oh, I'm so sorry. Is the ... is the phone
55 that's saying it's over, is that ... is that the 4, uh, is it the 957-6521 number, Ms. Bradley?

CALLER: Uh-huh.

AGENT: Oh, OK. Well, ma'am here. Just to explain to you. We're so sorry for any confusion. You're not
60 over your minutes yet on your number. Everything is set up correctly. You're not being charged for off-peak minutes, and you're not being charged for cell phone to cell phone calls. What the system was referring to was um ... minutes you went over
65 on the other number, 564-8482, since you don't have the text messaging service.

CALLER: Oh, we don't text message.

AGENT: Um, have you received any –

CALLER: Never text ... nah ... we don't text
70 message at all.

AGENT: What about receiving, because it's also counted. That's what the system is referring to. You, or rather your husband, actually used a number of text messages. That's what the system
75 is telling us.

CALLER: No, we don't even know how to do that. Come on!

AGENT: No, incoming, ma'am. Let's see on his phone. Do you think he's getting like, any text
80 messages at all from other people? 'Cause that is already counted, Ms. Bradley.

CALLER: No, because if he is, it's a mistake, because he doesn't know how to text messages

at all. We don't, we don't even do that. Neither
85 of us can work out that texting stuff.

AGENT: Oh, I do understand, ma'am. But like what I said, even if you don't do text messages, Ms. Bradley, let's say some of the people you know send you a message, it's also counted. Like your
90 kids, for example or –

CALLER: No, we don't have any. We don't text message and nobody text messages us.

AGENT: Um … oh, I understand. Well, here ma'am, just so we could make sure … and … like
95 what I've said, you're not over your voice minutes in total for both months. You've only used 70 of those as of today. As of this month.

CALLER: Yeah, I thought so.

AGENT: And then I'm going to put a block on
100 the text message just to make sure you won't be charged for this. Then I'll look into this problem further, Ms. Bradley. Is that OK?

CALLER: OK, and could you go back um … two months and see if that's what they have done,
105 because my bill was over 130 minutes and we've used the phone for two and a half years. We've never gone over before. And I couldn't figure it out, you know, what was going on. And um yeah, I paid $139 and I'm like I don't know why the bill
110 was over, because whenever, I mean, you know, we call each other, but we never go over the minutes. I don't know what happened to him!

AGENT: Oh … OK. Let's see. Was the bill last month for $130?

115 **CALLER:** Yeah.

AGENT: The June bill, right?

CALLER: Yeah, June, it was June.

AGENT: OK, well yeah, Ms. Bradley, from what see uh what I'm seeing on this bill, the charges or the
120 additional charges are coming from … additional minutes used, for both phones. You've used a total of 1,200 "anytime" minutes. That's where the additional charges are coming from.

CALLER: Yeah.

125 **AGENT:** And … let me see. What about on your phone, ma'am? Ah, like, let's see is the phone on roaming? Any of that Ms. Bradley?

CALLER: No.

AGENT: OK, the 6521 phone has also gone over
130 800 minutes on text messages coming in. So would you like to block messages on your phone, too?

CALLER: Oh, OK. So you could … you could block that so it doesn't do that anymore?

135 **AGENT:** Yeah, that's correct Ms. Bradley. Would you like me to block that on both phones?

CALLER: Yeah.

AGENT: OK, so you're the one who's using the 6521 phone, Ms. Bradley?

140 **CALLER:** Yes, ma'am.

AGENT: OK. Just give me one moment … OK, there you go, ma'am. I've already put a block on the text messaging. That's going to be for both incoming and outgoing messaging on both
145 phones. [That's good.] Just to make sure that you'll not rake up any further charges. So there you go, ma'am. Is there anything else I can assist you with today?

CALLER: Oh no. That's good. Thank you so
150 much.

AGENT: All right, just a quick recap. Again, I've blocked text messages on both of your numbers. And again, you've only used 70 minutes this month out of the 800 as of today. OK?

155 **CALLER:** Just one question. Do you know who, I mean, do you have a record of what numbers are texting us? Is it in this city?

AGENT: Oh, I have no record of that, I'm sorry.

CALLER: Just curious, 'cause they sure cost us.
160 Thanks anyway.

AGENT: You're welcome, ma'am, and have a good day today, and thanks for calling Fast Phones.

CALLER: Yes. Bye.

Additional Listening D1

1. We don't **text** message at all.
2. **We** don't text message at all.
3. Can you open the **door**?
4. Can **you** open the door?

UNIT 7

AGENT: Customer service, this is Dale. How can I help you?

CALLER: Ah, good morning. This is Lou Johnson calling. Who am I talking to?

5 **AGENT:** Dale. D-A-L-E.

CALLER: Pardon me?

AGENT: Dale.

CALLER: Dell?

AGENT: Dale. D-A-L-E

10 **CALLER:** Dale – Dell?

AGENT: That's right.

CALLER: OK. I'm calling in reference to my policy.

AGENT: Um … What's the –

15 **CALLER:** My life insurance policy.

AGENT: Yeah. Could you please give me your policy number?

CALLER: Yeah, that's uh 232-41-56L as in Lou.

AGENT: And your name please?

20 **CALLER:** Pardon me?

AGENT: Your name?

CALLER: Lou R. Johnson

AGENT: And how can I help you with this policy, sir?

25 **CALLER:** I received a termination notice.

AGENT: OK. Mmm let me check this out.

CALLER: This happens every month when your company is authorized to draw payment for my insurance from my bank account. And uh … are
30 you still there?

AGENT: I'm still here. I'm just looking into this …

CALLER: Yeah, and on November 16th we sent a letter in … to Customer Service … in reference to this practice … that is uh just causing us stress. And
35 we don't understand why you incorrectly draw off one amount when you should be drawing the higher amount, because we've authorized you for direct payment from the bank. You actually have the authorization to do so.

40 **AGENT:** I'm going to –

CALLER: Can you just, not you personally, can you … can you send notice of terminations … on non-payment?

AGENT: Hello, sir?

45 **CALLER:** Yeah?

AGENT: OK. Thank you so much for waiting. What is your phone number please?

CALLER: Area code 245-758-7785.

AGENT: OK, we receive a letter here. OK, I'm
50 going to … OK … what I'm going to do right now, sir … I'm going to put this to our Reinstatement Department. I'm going to let them check this record of yours. If they could put this to automatic reinstatement.

55 **CALLER:** I'm sorry. Would you repeat, sir? I'm … I'm sorry …

AGENT: Uh, I'm going –

CALLER: Hello?

AGENT: I'm going to put this to our
60 Reinstatement Department.

CALLER: Which de–? Which department?

AGENT: Reinstatement. And they'll be the one to check the record … if they could put the policy back in force again. Because there is actually a

65 letter here, so that is justification. We need to review the documents here, if that is sufficient.

CALLER: So … so, which … so it's going to which department now?

AGENT: Reinstatement Department.

70 **CALLER:** Statement Department?

AGENT: Reinstatement Department.

CALLER: Statement Department?

AGENT: Reinstatement. R-E-I-N-S-T-A-M-E-N-T. Reinstatement Department.

75 **CALLER:** All right. That's re-, re-, re- what? Reinstatement?

AGENT: You've got it correctly right now!

CALLER: OK. Thank you.

AGENT: So … I'm just going to make a request
80 here. Um. It'll be looked into by that department. [Uh-huh.] So you're still going to hear from us, whatever the decision is in this case.

CALLER: Do you have my November 16th letter?

AGENT: Yes, I do have that.

85 **CALLER:** It was very clear. They are authorized to withdraw from the bank account the payments that are required to pay for this policy.

AGENT: I'm going to put that as a justification.

CALLER: Yeah. And in the past they were
90 withdrawing the incorrect amount, and we authorized them to draw down the correct amount, the increased amount. I still have tons of letters here back and forwards … on termination. Every time something happens they send a
95 termination, which sends my wife through the ceiling, and myself. Causes us distress. You can understand that, I'm sure you can, you sound like a reasonable person.

AGENT: Uh-huh. Uh, right now –

100 **CALLER:** I don't understand what the incompetence is at all. I mean, it's not you personally, Mr. Dell.

AGENT: I understand, sir. Right now, sir, uh … what we're withdrawing on your letter is uh
105 $1,155. But the cost of insurance here, let me see, is already recent because it's past your anniversary date. It's $1,270. It's like that amount. If you're willing to –

CALLER: 1,000 what? 207?

110 **AGENT:** $1,276.

CALLER: $1,276. Why didn't they draw that amount?

AGENT: So, if you're willing to do that, I'm going to make a justification –

115 **CALLER:** I'm willing to do that! They have authorization to pay the premiums from my

account! I mean, why is someone not drawing the correct amount? Because I don't send any money to you. You automatically are supposed
120 to withdraw the payments from the account! I'm not yelling at you, sir. Please understand that, Mr. Dell. Someone's goofing up there and putting me through stress! Somebody's got a case of incompetence. I have never actually
125 sent the payment directly from my house in the mail to you guys. No! You can automatically draw it out of the bank account. And the money is always there.

AGENT: Let me see –

130 **CALLER:** In fact, excuse me, do you have a copy of the November 30th letter that you sent me of termination?

AGENT: Yes, sir.

CALLER: It makes no mention of any amount
135 of money that was due. It's just a stereotypical letter!

AGENT: Yes, sir. Uh –

CALLER: It does not say you failed to pay $1,276.

AGENT: Yes, sir. But to keep ... to ... to still keep
140 the policy in force right now ... Let me see ... because the policy has canceled out ... Let me see ... Because the policy has canceled out, what we'll draft there is about initially ... $2,881 ... It's the initial. And then after that, it's amounting to
145 about ... $1,270 every month to keep the policy ongoing. So if you wanted to do that, I'm going to make such justification to our Reinstatement Department.

CALLER: Thank you!

150 **AGENT:** Uh-huh.

CALLER: I appreciate that very much. I just don't want to have to go to my lawyers on all of these goof ups. ... Mr. Dell?

AGENT: Yes, sir.

155 **CALLER:** This has been going on for over a year and a half, almost two years. I have documentation of all these errors that have been made by my insurance company. I've talked to numerous different representatives on this, to kind of
160 straighten it up. And every time what turns up is, you – well, not you, Dell – but someone else there, you send me the same type of stereotypical letter notifying me of termination. I don't send money or checks! Someone is failing to do their job.

165 **AGENT:** OK, actually, I'm going to make just such justifications. It's already been done, sir. We just need to wait for their decision in that case.

CALLER: And in addition to sending me these termination letters, every time they withdraw,
170 why don't they just send me a letter saying, "We've withdrawn this amount of money as payment for your premiums"? Common sense!

AGENT: Yes, sir. I understand. So we'll just have to wait for the decision. I've already made your
175 justification on your end.

CALLER: OK. How am I gonna be notified?

AGENT: You'll be notified through writing, or if not, someone from that department will call you.

CALLER: OK, OK, thank you very much and have
180 a blessed weekend.

AGENT: You, too, sir. Bye-bye.

UNIT 8

AGENT: Thank you for calling Lensolutions Technical Support. My name is Ivy. May I have your phone number associated with your Lensolutions account, please? Thank you for calling Lensolutions
5 Technical Support. Hello?

CALLER: Hello?

AGENT: Hello there. Yes, sir. My name is Ivy. And I'm going to need to have your area code and phone number so I can show your Lensolutions
10 account.

CALLER: OK. So area code 095. Phone 6387-9021.

AGENT: Thank you. And your email address, please?

15 **CALLER:** Yeah, that's uh Nicholas at greatwall dot com.

AGENT: That's correct. And your name, please? Just so I'm able to –

CALLER: Nicholas Marks.

20 **AGENT:** All right. And yes ... how can I help you tonight?

CALLER: Well, I received a disc from Lensolutions QQQ for the Internet. [Yes.] And I'm not able to get online.

25 **AGENT:** So what we're trying to accomplish is for you is to install that CD so that you can get on to the internet. If we can achieve that today, I'll be happy!

CALLER: Yeah, so will I. I went through the system
30 and I don't know where the problem lies. And when I signed up, I asked them about what I'm gonna be doing before. And they should know.

AGENT: All right. Let me explain something. You have an account with us. The fact is that you do
35 have an account with us and you'll be billed. [Yes.] But putting in that CD and registering your primary email account will not charge you anything.

CALLER: Oh, that's not what she said, and I don't like paying for service that I can't even get on.

40 **AGENT:** Let me help you go online, sir. Are we calling you on the second telephone line?

CALLER: No.

AGENT: Oh. One line. Let me take a look here. Is this computer running on Jive or 2001?

45 **CALLER:** Uh … I think it's Jive.

AGENT: Jive. All right. Thank you. Are there any bird icons on the desktop? The one that looks like a bird or anything that has the name Lensolutions?

CALLER: Yes, it does.

50 **AGENT:** What's the name of that bird icon?

CALLER: Just Lensolutions.

AGENT: Just Lensolutions. All right. So you have already installed that Lensolutions QQQ disc. Please … double click that icon, please.

55 **CALLER:** Yes, I did that already. It says Lensolutions Messenger. Now I sign in, right?

AGENT: Lensolutions Messenger. All right. Lensolutions Messenger is actually a separate complementary program. And if you log on using
60 Lensolutions Messenger, it'll not sign us in. Uh, it'll not get us online, is what I mean by that. Let's close it, please. Let's try this one instead. Press the Start button. [Uh-huh.] Then click on Run. [On Run?] Correct. [OK.] And please type in L-E-N. Then
65 press OK. What do we see on the screen?

CALLER: OK. Now it's my email. This is log on L-E-N –

AGENT: OK. Let's do something else. But first I want you to sign in. If it starts to dial up, click the
70 Cancel button.

CALLER: It doesn't say Dialup. It says, uh, type the password.

AGENT: Oh yeah, that's what I need. Type in the password first. Then press Sign-in and it'll start
75 to dial up, but just stay with me, and when it is dialing a number, press Cancel.

CALLER: OK. So uh now that I type in my password. Put in Sign-in?

AGENT: Yes, please. OK, there. Is it showing a
80 phone number?

CALLER: Yes.

AGENT: OK. That's great. So you're done here. Press Cancel first. Uh what may have –

CALLER: It says we did not detect a dial tone
85 except for your dialing.

AGENT: Exactly. Because we are using this phone line. But the reason why I ask you to sign in first is to make sure that we go to Dialup after this call. The next thing that we need to do is erase that
90 confusion where that LEN bird is. And delete your LEN icon on the desktop? [OK.] All right. Click the icon. [Uh-huh.] And left click on –

CALLER: LEN?

AGENT: No, sir. Please click on Delete.

95 **CALLER:** OK. So click on the icon. Right click on the LEN icon?

AGENT: Correct.

CALLER: Press Delete.

AGENT: That's right.

100 **CALLER:** OK, confirm Shortcut Delete.

AGENT: Yes. So that's a shortcut. To get the correct shortcut, we can press the Start button.

CALLER: Uh-huh …

AGENT: Then click on –

105 **CALLER:** Run?

AGENT: No, not this time, sir. Just click on All Programs. Look for anything that says LEN only. Just LEN … Have we located it?

CALLER: Uh … no.

110 **AGENT:** Oh. No. OK, let's try this one then. Uh right click the Start button.

CALLER: Right click Start button.

AGENT: And left click on Properties.

CALLER: Yeah, I tried that before, I think.

115 **AGENT:** Good, so … we should be in the Start properties. Make sure that the dot is on the first option Start manual. Then click Customized.

CALLER: Done that.

AGENT: And then at the bottom you should have
120 shown on Start manual, we should have a check mark beside Internet.

CALLER: Yes, it does.

AGENT: And the right side and across it should be LEN.

125 **CALLER:** Yup.

AGENT: OK. That's it. Press Cancel.

CALLER: OK. Doesn't it need to be on check mark on Email as well?

AGENT: We can bring the check mark beside
130 Email if you want to, or … change that to LEN as well.

CALLER: OK. Double check marks and enables LEN.

AGENT: That's great. Then let's press Cancel.
135 [OK.] And Cancel again. [OK.] Try this, this time. Press the Start button. [Mmm-hmm.] And that's only after on the left corner of your screen you see Internet LEN. [Uh-huh.] Press that, please. And it should give us the same screen. [Yup.] All right.
140 And is there anything else I can help you with?

CALLER: No, it seems it's luck that I can do it now. Uh, you sound mighty young and you can do it all …

12

AGENT: No, you're doing great. So, uh you'll
145 go on LEN. I'm sure that it's just that when we
double click the icon, it pulls up LEN messenger,
and ... that one requires you should be online first
before we actually sign in. So ... [OK.] I'll be leaving
a note on your account. So the next person will
150 be aware of what we've discussed so far, if they
access that note. And thank you for calling LEN.

CALLER: Thank you.

AGENT: No problem with that. Have a great day
to you. Bye-bye.

155 **CALLER:** Thank you. Bye-bye.

Additional Listening D1 (1)

AGENT: What seems to be the problem, sir?
CALLER: Well, my monitor is blurry.
AGENT: Have you tried turning it off and on
again?
5 **CALLER:** Yes, I have and it's still blurry.
AGENT: I see. Then go to the panel at the bottom
of the monitor and open it.
CALLER: OK, and then ...?

Additional Listening D1 (2)

A: I have something I need to tell you.
B: What is it?
A: I'm moving to another country.
B: Really?

UNIT 9

AGENT: Good afternoon, Customer Service. My
name is Denise. May I have your policy number
please?

CALLER: OK. I just called about 30 minutes ago
5 and the girl told me to call back in 30 minutes. I
don't have a policy number. I have a contract
number.

AGENT: Yes, ma'am. May I have your contract
number please?

10 **CALLER:** 548-9111.

AGENT: That's 548-9111?

CALLER: Yes.

AGENT: That policy number is not coming up
in our system, ma'am. Are you the owner of the
15 policy?

CALLER: OK. Let's go through this one more
time. All right, I repeat the letter from you, it says
to Barbara Anne Fowler Jones, my address, my
account, my zip code, and the next thing says
20 the contract number. Insured: Robert M. Fowler,
who is my father. You sent me the letter, you've
called me twice this week, so now I'm calling to

find out what you want, and you tell me "we don't
have nothing". Well, somebody said something
25 somewhere.

AGENT: OK, um, on the cover does it say on the
letterhead ... does it say Standard Insurance Life
or Standard Insurance Life and Accident, ma'am?

CALLER: It says Standard Insurance Life.

30 **AGENT:** What is the last name of your father,
ma'am?

CALLER: Robert M. Fowler. F-O-W-L-E-R.

AGENT: And his date of birth, ma'am?

CALLER: OK. I don't know. August 23rd ... August
35 24th ... I don't know his Social Security number,
you know. All I have are the papers you sent me,
and I'm the beneficiary – or one of the many ... If
it tells you anything, it says Claims Department,
then it says C-O-R-R and then it has the number,
40 and then it says a carbon copy to Michael
Cunningham, whoever he is.

AGENT: OK, just a moment, ma'am. I'm trying to
make an alpha search for the name of your father.
Um but I'll need his date of birth to be able to
45 narrow down the search.

CALLER: You guys should have that, you know.
I don't have that. I know it's August 23rd, 24th, but
I don't know what year. He's probably 83, I don't
know.

50 **AGENT:** OK, because actually, ma'am, there's a
lot of Robert Fowlers coming up in the system, so
for me to be able to segregate it, I'll need his date
of birth.

CALLER: Search the one that says August 23rd,
55 24th. I mean you guys have called me twice
this week. You know someone wants me. You
sent me a check for $9.92 – opposed to sending
me a check for $500. Now, how did you come
up with $9.92? Ah, I shouldn't have paid for the
60 policy.

AGENT: Just let me check, ma'am. One moment,
please. OK. I was able to trace the policy. I'm
just checking on the documentation here.
One moment, please. OK, well actually, ma'am,
65 I'm seeing here a check for $9.92 was issued
um ... there was actually a discrepancy of the
original check that was sent over for you on this
one.

CALLER: Uh-huh?

70 **AGENT:** And the re-issued check ... the re-issued
check sent over was lacking $9.92, and that's
the reason you were sent over another check for
$9.92.

CALLER: I don't understand. I got a check for
75 $9.92.

AGENT: Actually, ma'am, before that there was a
check that was sent out for $842.

CALLER: To who? I didn't get no check for $800.

13

AGENT: I'm seeing here, ma'am, that a check
80 was sent over for Barbara Anne F. Jones at 452
Meadow Lane –

CALLER: I did not get a check for $800! All I've
received, which I haven't cashed yet, is a check for
$9.92. I've never received an $800 check.

85 **AGENT:** Well, we actually have a copy of –

CALLER: OK. We need to find out where it went. I
never cashed a check for $800. You need to put a
tracer on it, and find out whose signature is on it;
'cause I never cashed it. I never got one!

90 **AGENT:** OK, I'm seeing here, ma'am that it was
sent over to 452 Meadow Lane –

CALLER: OK. I live at 452 Meadow Lane! I never
received a check!

AGENT: OK, well, the most I can do is to have this
95 one sent over for further research, because we are
seeing here the check with a signature on it.

CALLER: OK, give me a copy of that check back so
I can send it to some law – or somebody because
somebody cashed it and I never got it!

100 **AGENT:** OK, may I have your daytime phone
number please, ma'am?

CALLER: Area code 371-654-7897 – that's a cell
number.

AGENT: OK, I'll have this sent over to the proper
105 department for research. Is there anything else I
can help you with today?

CALLER: Why have you been calling me this
week? Do we know that answer? I mean if you
hadn't called me, I wouldn't have been calling
110 you, would I?

AGENT: One moment please. [Yep.] We called
actually just to verify the address, ma'am.

CALLER: To verify the address?

AGENT: Uh, your address, ma'am.

115 **CALLER:** For what?

AGENT: To send over the check, ma'am.

CALLER: What check? I got the $9.92 check!

AGENT: Um Ms. Jones. OK. I'll need to ask you to
please stop shouting because I am trying to help
120 you on this.

CALLER: You know what? At this point, that's
probably the most ridiculous thing you could tell
me because I'm being patient. You guys don't
have any answers.

125 **AGENT:** I'm just reading to what … what is
actually documented here on our records,
ma'am.

CALLER: OK, they've called me twice and all I'm
asking is why did they call me and you're saying
130 to verify my address! Oh, I shouldn't have even
bothered to!

AGENT: Yes, ma'am. That's correct. I'm seeing
here and I'm going to read you verbatim the
documentation. OK? "Called and left message
135 for Barbara Anne Fowler Jones. Needs to verify
address." It's exactly what is written on our
documentation.

CALLER: But you said you had an address because
you sent me an $800 check.

140 **AGENT:** That's probably the reason why we
needed to verify the address.

CALLER: But you sent me the $9.92 check at that
address, which I received and which I haven't
cashed.

145 **AGENT:** The Claims Department … that is the
only documentation they placed on it. They called
and left a message.

CALLER: I probably need to talk to someone
higher up. Because if you're sending me a check
150 and somebody cashed it, then I need to know.
I need to talk to somebody higher up!

AGENT: That's the reason why I'm putting this in
for further research, ma'am.

CALLER: OK, there's nobody else I can talk to?

155 **AGENT:** No, ma'am. Is there anything else I can
help you with today?

CALLER: There's nobody else in that office that is
higher up than you?

AGENT: Our supervisor is currently in a meeting
160 right now, ma'am.

CALLER: OK, then I need to leave a number for
the supervisor to call me back ASAP, because this
answer you're giving me is not flying.

AGENT: Ma'am, we are going to have this
165 one placed into further research by Claims
Department. Anything else?

CALLER: OK. At the moment I'll be out by $800
because somebody's cashed – signed my name to
a check that I know nothing about.

170 **AGENT:** And that's the reason why I'm putting
this for further research, ma'am. I'm going to be
reporting this one … that you did not receive
the check. However we've received a copy of the
encashed check.

175 **CALLER:** OK, I need to know what your name is.

AGENT: My name is Denise, ma'am.

CALLER: Denise. Denise what?

AGENT: Castro. C for Charlie, A for Alpha, S for
Sierra, T for Tango, R for Romeo, O for Oscar.

180 **CALLER:** OK. And your supervisor's name?

AGENT: We're not allowed to give out that
information, ma'am.

CALLER: What are my hours to talk to this
supervisor?

AGENT: I'm sorry, ma'am?

CALLER: This is a big insurance company and you only have one person. Who is this Michael Cunningham?

AGENT: I'm not aware of that name, ma'am.

190 **CALLER:** OK. He's on your paperwork … which would be cc, carbon copy to Michael Cunningham, 65482 Business Street, Stevens, Iowa.

AGENT: Let me just check that one, ma'am. One moment please. I'm seeing here Michael
195 Cunningham is the servicing agent for this particular policy.

CALLER: Then I need his telephone number.

AGENT: One moment please.

CALLER: I'll call him myself. Oh, I'd love to put
100 someone in jail for this!

UNIT 10

AGENT: Thank you for calling AXE Financial Services. This is Carol. May I have your account number please?

CALLER: 756-845-7758.

5 **AGENT:** OK, let me just repeat, it's 756-845-7758. Is that correct?

CALLER: Uh-huh.

AGENT: Thank you so much. One moment, and let me just pull up the account. May I have your
10 full name please?

CALLER: Jane Groundling.

AGENT: OK, how do you spell your last name?

CALLER: G-R-O-U-N for Nelly, D for David L-I-N-G.

15 **AGENT:** Thank you, and for verification purposes, may I know the company name you're calling for and your billing zip code?

CALLER: It's Fitwell Construction 98766.

AGENT: I see, Miss Groundling. [Ms. please.] OK,
20 I'm sorry, Ms. Groundling, Fitwell Construction is showing in my record as a billing business, but … this is not the name of the account.

CALLER: Fitwell Construction Ltd. Please put me through to the supervisor immediately. I've
25 already called here so many times, and I need to get the matter rectified immediately.

AGENT: Yes, I understand that, ma'am. Um maybe I could help you. How may I help you?

CALLER: Probably not, because I had to go to the
30 supervisor before. It's got to do with the name. That's the problem. No one seems to be able to work out the right account on my payment. I spend half my life on the phone with you guys!

AGENT: I'm sorry to hear that. Do you mean the
35 name on this account?

CALLER: Correct.

AGENT: OK.

CALLER: I'm only the contact person … and … you put me in my husband's name on the
40 invoice.

AGENT: But let me just verify this, Ms. Groundling. You're um in this account, the contact person is actually, yours … you. It's … this … it's the account … the contact person is under your
45 name. And you want it to be changed under your husband's name?

CALLER: Well, it should be under my husband's name, Fitwell Construction Ltd. I've made this request so many times and nothing ever happens.
50 [Hmm.] It had our personal names.

AGENT: Uh because we can actually change this … account name –

CALLER: But they haven't. If they were changing it, they would've done it by now, and they
55 would've sent me a new invoice, which has not happened.

AGENT: Did you fill out any change form?

CALLER: No, I didn't.

AGENT: 'Cause in order for you to –

60 **CALLER:** This is not the first time we've bought a computer from you people, but I can tell you it might be the last.

AGENT: We do apologize, ma'am. However, ma'am, in order for us to change the name, you
65 need to fill out this form, a name change form, and … I'll … I can –

CALLER: This is not a name change, ma'am. This is a company. We've been in business for several years now, and this shouldn't be an issue.

70 **AGENT:** Because for this account, ma'am, this account is under the name of Harry Stead Junior, but if … since you would like this account to be under the name of Fitwell Construction. [Mm-hmm.] We can do that. And in order for us to
75 change the name of this account, a name-change form needs to be filled out.

CALLER: And what would that do?

AGENT: Hello, I'm sorry.

CALLER: What would that do?

80 **AGENT:** This will change the name under the … put it under … Fitwell Construction. You just need to fill it out and send it back to us, and it'll be one billing cycle to take effect.

CALLER: Take how long?

85 **AGENT:** One billing cycle to take effect. So the next input –

CALLER: One billing cycle? This is … this is … the 60 days … 60 days? I sent out my payment out today. Do whatever it is you need to, but let me
90 speak to your supervisor in the interim.

AGENT: OK, one moment, let me just check on that … Thank you for waiting. Hello, ma'am? Ms. Groundling? Ms. Groundling? Hello? Hello?

CALLER: Yes.

95 **AGENT:** Yes, Ms. Groundling. Yes, unfortunately, ma'am, my supervisor is still engaged on the phone call right now.

CALLER: Oh, OK, well, I called over a week ago. And, nobody ever returned my call regarding the
100 name of this, and it seems a big major problem, and we've bought … purchased the computer under the business name … before, so why …

AGENT: Yeah.

CALLER: And now, that's the problem now?
105 And now you're telling me I have to change the name, and I spoke to your supervisor in your department over a week ago and nobody has ever said anything about that, and now you're telling me it's as simple as a form with the company
110 name Fitwell Construction. Where will it end? In tears no doubt!

AGENT: I can understand that, I mean, how you feel.

CALLER: So, uh if that supervisor is not available,
115 who would her boss be?

AGENT: OK, um, I do apologize, Ms. Groundling. I've just seen in your account that you talked to one of our representatives, a Mr. Smith, your local rep down on … Fed Street. He … he has reported
120 a name change, but –

CALLER: No, I've already called him. They can't do anything locally. They said they couldn't do anything 'cause they only have us down as Fitwell Construction. They don't have … they
125 don't have our personal names, they only have our business name.

AGENT: OK, here's what we will do, Ms. Groundling. We will forward your issue to our Resolution Team and they will call you –

130 **CALLER:** They already did that, ma'am. OK? That was over a week ago when I called the first time.

AGENT: Were you given a case number for that?

CALLER: I was given a case number. I don't
135 know if it's correct. It's 45678.

AGENT: And, did you receive a call from our Resolution Team?

CALLER: No, I didn't. I haven't received any call from anybody.

140 **AGENT:** OK.

CALLER: That's the problem. You see I keep phoning and I get a different story every time I call.

AGENT: OK, let me check our supervisor again.
145 One moment, please … Thank you for waiting, Ms. Groundling. [Yes.] Ms. Groundling, here's what we will do, ma'am. We will transfer your call to the Authorized Solution Department. Will that be fine?

150 **CALLER:** I really don't know how to answer that question. Resolution Team, Authorized Solution Department. They sound good, but what do they do?

AGENT: We'll have the issue resolved right away
155 at ASD, and since you said earlier that you did not receive any calls [Nope.] on [Nope.] from the Resolution Department. [No, I did not.] What I will do, ma'am, is to transfer your call to the department.

160 **CALLER:** OK.

AGENT: Will … will there be anything else that I can assist you with before I transfer your call?

CALLER: No.

AGENT: OK.

165 **CALLER:** Thank you very much.

AGENT: You're very welcome. Please stay on the line and I'll transfer your call.

CALLER: OK.

The calls in this course are all based on authentic call center interactions. The language used by the caller and agent have not been changed except when they relate to products or sensitive information. This is why zip codes and phone numbers may not follow conventions. Grammar and other mistakes made by callers and agents have been left uncorrected.